AMERICA'S PAST:

A NEW WORLD ARCHAEOLOGY

THOMAS C. PATTERSON

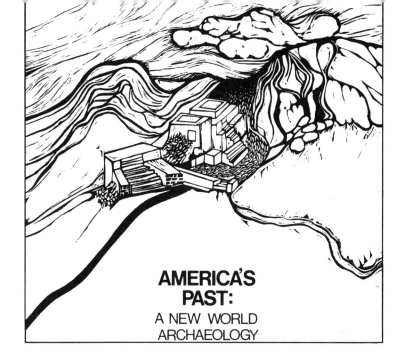

AMERICA'S PAST:
A NEW WORLD ARCHAEOLOGY

THOMAS C. PATTERSON
Department of Anthropology
Temple University

Scott, Foresman and Company
Glenview, Illinois   London

Library of Congress Catalog Card No: 74-188619
ISBN: 0-673-05273-7

Copyright © 1973 by Scott, Foresman and Company,
Glenview, Illinois 60025
Philippines Copyright 1973 by Scott, Foresman and Company.
All Rights Reserved. Printed in the United States of America.
Regional offices of Scott, Foresman and Company are
located in Dallas, Oakland, N.J., Palo Alto, and Tucker, Ga.

For Jack Goins,
who first showed me what anthropology was about

Preface

The intent of this book is to introduce students—both beginning and advanced—to New World archaeology. This could be done in various ways. The book might consist of a series of regional archaeological syntheses examining the cultural history of large areas—such as the Amazon Basin, Texas, or the eastern United States. Or it might describe the cultures that existed in different areas at any particular moment in the past—perhaps four thousand years ago—and the relationships between them. However, there are difficulties with both the regional and cross-cultural approaches.

The first is the unevenness of our information. The archaeological records of some areas—like the central coast of Peru or the Tehuacán Valley of Mexico—are relatively complete, while those of other regions—Patagonia or lower Central America, for example—are very poorly known. We have a good deal of information about what happened in the central Andes before 2000 B.C. and virtually none about the same period in the Amazon Basin. In general, we have more information from areas where intensive archaeological investigations have been carried out. However, the variation in our knowledge also reflects circumstances beyond the archaeologist's control—for example, the preservation conditions in the area where he works or the amount of site destruction that has occurred. A second difficulty with the regional and cross-cultural approaches is space. To describe the archaeology of every region in the New World, even superficially, would require a book many times the length of this one.

Instead, I have focused on a series of problems in American archaeology: the entry of man into the New World, the development of food-producing economies in various areas, some consequences of permanent settlement, the formation of states, and some ecological implications of different economic strategies and population pressures. We could have chosen other questions, such as the kinds of cultural adaptations that emerged in different areas after the end of the Pleistocene Epoch, whether or not there were culturally significant contacts between the Old World and the New before A.D. 1500, or the consequences of European conquest and economic domination of the native American peoples during the past five centuries.

Unfortunately, this choice of problems produces a very unequal coverage of the archaeology of different areas in the New World. Some regions are examined in considerable detail, while others are hardly or never mentioned. Even though I have tried to use data from as many regions as possible, the emphasis of this book preselects areas where relevant archaeological evidence is available and ignores others, even though a great deal may be known about them. For example, a lot has been written about the agricultural practices of the ancient Maya, but, in fact, there is *no* archaeological evidence that tells us about the plant foods these groups ate before the sixteenth century or how they grew these crops. The only data that bear directly on this question come from a few pollen cores taken in a part of the Maya area where no archaeological research has been carried out.

The problems I chose to examine not only interest me personally but also have considerable theoretical importance. Archaeologists working in both hemispheres have made significant contributions to our understanding of them. We will consider one of these problems in each chapter, after a brief introduction to our subject in Chapter One.

I did not write this book for my colleagues in American archaeology; however, I also could not have written it without the help that many of them gave so freely. Since many individuals have contributed to my understanding of the problems discussed in this book, it is easiest to acknowledge their help and to thank them for it in terms of the chapters I have written. *Chapter One:* Richard Gould, Edward Lanning, John Rowe, Karen Spalding, and Gary Vescelius; *Chapter Two:* Junius Bird, Alan Bryan, William Byrne, Don Crabtree, George Denton, Kent Flannery, Bruce Grove, Kensaku Hayashi, Wesley Hurt, William Irving, Cynthia Irwin-Williams, Henry Irwin, Frederick Johnson, Edward Lanning, George MacDonald, Richard MacNeish, James Millar, Karen Spalding, Claude Warren, Hurd Willett, and Edwin Wilmsen; *Chapter Three:* William Allen, Jacques Barrau, Lewis Binford, William Byrne, Eric Callen, Edward Calnek, C. D. Darlington, James Fitting, Kent Flannery, Verne Grant, David Harris, J. C. Hawkes, John Henderson, Nichlas Hellmuth, Lawrence Kaplan, Edward Lanning, Donald Lathrap, Thomas Lynch, Richard MacNeish, Ramón Margalef, Michael Moseley, Barbara Pickersgill, Barbara Price, Timothy Prout, Rudolfo Ruibal, Carl Sauer, Janet Siskind, Karen Spalding, Karen Stothert, Stuart

Struever, and Elizabeth Wing. *Chapter Four:* Edward Calnek, Michael Coe, Jorge Flores, William Isbell, Eugene McDougle, René Millon, Craig Morris, Michael Moseley, John Murra, Barbara Price, Rogger Ravines, Janet Suskind, and Karen Spalding. *Chapter Five:* Edward Calnek, Carlo Cipolla, Christopher Donnan, Kent Flannery, John Henderson, William Isbell, Edward Lanning, Richard MacNeish, Dorothy Menzel, René Millon, John Murra, Angel Palerm, Louise Paradis, Lee Parsons, Barbara Price, Rogger Ravines, John Rowe, Janet Suskind, Karen Spalding, Paul Tolstoy, Gary Vescelius, Eric Wolf, Judith Zeitlin, and Robert Zeitlin. *Chapter Six:* Linda De Laurentis, Bruce Grove, Helen Moses, John Murra, Janet Siskind, Karen Spalding, George Vlach, Irving Winters, Judith Zeitlin, and Robert Zeitlin. This book probably would not have been completed without their help and encouragement and without the assistance of Nancy Kannappan, my editor at Scott, Foresman and Company.

Thomas C. Patterson

Contents

1. What Is Archaeology?

ARCHAEOLOGY AND HISTORY

We cannot directly observe what happened in the past. We cannot watch the impact that agriculture had on the inhabitants of Mexico in the fifth millennium B.C. or see the effects of the Spanish conquest on the natives of Peru in the sixteenth century A.D. We can, however, learn a great deal about these and other events that happened long ago by digging up and studying the remains left by ancient peoples. Bringing the past back to life by studying ancient remains is the business of archaeology.

At first, this definition of archaeology may seem a little vague. Still, it is really not such a bad definition, because it is broad enough to encompass the activities of all sorts of people who find it essential to use archaeological evidence to clarify and explain what happened in the past. An archaeologist is not only a person who digs up ancient garbage dumps to learn about the changes that agricultural production brought in Mexico; he is also one who excavates a native chief's house in Peru to verify and elaborate on what a Spanish census-taker wrote about the man in the sixteenth century. What makes both archaeologists is that they are using evidence that was not consciously left for posterity by the peoples they are trying to understand.

Archaeologists, of course, are not the only people trying to understand and explain what happened in the past. Historians rightly claim that they too are doing just that. It is clear that the goals of the archaeologist and the historian are very similar, even though the particular problems they study may be very different. It is also clear that most archaeologists are not historians and that most historians are not archaeologists. If it is not their aims that distinguish them, what does? Many distinctions have been suggested, but the only difference that stands up consistently under close examination is the one based on the kinds of evidence they use and the techniques they have developed for dealing with this information.

The historian deals almost exclusively with written records and reconstructs the past largely on the basis of what they say. Unfortunately, written evidence can be distorted in several ways. Until recently in some parts of the world, and even today in others, only a small segment of the population was literate, and our understanding of what happened is based on the views and biases of this group. Further, written records can contain errors of fact, introduced either accidentally or deliberately, and the historian has had to develop techniques for checking the accuracy of his evidence.

The archaeologist is not so concerned with the accuracy of views that ancient peoples had about themselves because he is dealing largely with things that were not intentionally left for the future—broken pottery in a garbage dump, a child and his toys buried in a circular pit, or an abandoned hilltop village. In reconstructing the past, the archaeologist uses such evidence for purposes very different from those of the people who left it. He does, however, have to worry about whether his evidence adequately reflects the activities that took place and, if not, what biases are distorting his information.

ARCHAEOLOGICAL EVIDENCE AND INTERPRETATION

Archaeological evidence is found at places where ancient peoples lived or performed some particular task, like quarrying rock for building materials or disposing of the dead.

Objects and Associations

We can distinguish two kinds of archaeological evidence: objects and associations. *Objects* are things that were made, modified, or moved by man. Objects that were manufactured or modified in some way are usually called *artifacts*—broken pieces of pottery vessels, for example, or a statue carved out of stone. Artifacts inform us about the artistic and technical skills of the people who made them and about other things as well, if we can determine how they were used.

We know, for example, that the people living on the central Peruvian coast about A.D. 1000 used a particular kind of round-bottomed pottery vessel, made in a two-piece horizontal mold, for cooking over open fires, even though we have found neither a complete vessel nor the mold in which one was made. We have found lots of fragments of such vessels. Pieces from the sides frequently show join lines where the molded clay sections were fitted together, and pieces from the bottoms are heavily sooted on the outside, often with thickly charred deposits on the interiors. If these charred deposits were analyzed microscopically, we might even be able to determine what was cooking when the pot broke.

Objects that were modified or altered in some way by man can also provide a great deal of information about the behavior of ancient peoples. We know, for example, that a major change in culinary techniques occurred on the central coast of Peru about two thousand years ago. Pits lined with fire-cracked rocks and filled with charcoal, ash, and charred seashells indicate that the population of this area had rather frequent clambakes before about 50 B.C. Fire-cracked rocks and charred seashells are virtually absent in sites after this date, in spite of the fact that both rocks and shells are just as common as they had been earlier. Another significant difference is that the later sites contain many more cooking pot fragments. This combination of facts suggests that the later peoples boiled their shellfish, probably in much the same way that their descendants do today.

Natural or unmodified objects found in archaeological sites also provide useful information about the past. To use another example from the central coast of Peru, a complete spondylus shell was found in an archaeological site occupied between six and seven thousand years ago. This species of marine shellfish lives only in the warm waters of the Equatorial Counter Current that flows along the coast of Ecuador and Colombia. Its presence in a site near Lurín, Peru furnishes excellent evidence for the existence of some sort of exchange system between populations that lived more than five hundred miles from each other.

The other kind of archaeological evidence consists of *associations*, which are the spatial relationships of objects with respect to each other and to features of the natural environment. There are many kinds of archaeological associations. The fact that tubular turquoise beads, bits of tapestry cloth, and fishing equipment were among the objects found with a man buried at Ancón, Peru is one. The fact that the beads were around his neck rather than his wrist or head is another. And the fact that his grave was located on a hill overlooking the ocean is still another.

Associations tell us a great deal about aspects of behavior that we would know nothing about if we only studied the objects found in an archaeological site. For many years, archaeologists working in the eastern United States puzzled about the use of certain flat, semicircular stones with a hole in the middle that they called bannerstones. The first bannerstones were collected without archaeological associations, and there was nothing about their shape that would tell us how they were used. After many years, an archaeologist excavated one in a burial and recorded its associations. The hole in the bannerstone was lined up with a bone spear-thrower hook, and its position with respect to the

3

hook indicated that it could only have been a spear-thrower weight, in spite of the fact that the wooden shaft of the spear-thrower had completely disintegrated with the passage of time.

Dating Archaeological Evidence

All the examples of associations just cited are of a particular kind, called *associations of contemporaneity,* which indicates that certain objects were used at the same time. In addition to objects found in graves, associations of contemporaneity can include such diverse remains as a house that burned down before its occupants could remove their possessions or the refuse thrown into a garbage dump for a very short period, such as a single season. Associations of contemporaneity are important, because they allow us to begin to group together those objects and associations that were characteristic of a particular time and place. The array of contemporary objects and associations found at an archaeological site is an *assemblage.* By examining the contents of an assemblage, we begin to describe the cultural patterns of the people who lived at that particular time and place and to compare them with those of peoples who lived earlier or later in the same area, or at the same time in other areas.

How do we know that a particular array of associations and objects found at one site is contemporary with assemblages found at different archaeological sites in the same area? The answer is based on the fact that things tend to change with the passage of time. Thus, for example, the style of pottery manufac-tured and used two thousand years ago on the central coast of Peru was very different from that made and used even two hundred years later. Consequently, vessels that are identical or very similar in shape and decoration probably have about the same age: if the archaeologist cannot distinguish significant differences between them, he treats them as equivalent in age.

Principles of Stratigraphy

Once he has determined that certain assemblages found at different sites in the same area are contemporary with each other because of similarities in their contents, how does the archaeolo-gist reconstruct the cultural patterns of an ancient people? Let us suppose, for a moment, that a very particular and distinctive form of pottery vessel is found in three different archaeological contexts: shaft and chamber tombs dug into alluvial fans along the bottoms of hills, storage pits in fortified villages on the tops of these hills, and garbage dumps immediately outside the walls of these settlements. Given these different associations, the archae-ologist can determine a great deal about the people who used the

4

vessel. He knows, for example, how and where they disposed of the dead, what offerings were placed in their graves, what kinds of buildings they made and used, what kinds of food they ate and, by inference, how they obtained their livelihood and something about the nature of their relations with other peoples. By grouping together contemporary assemblages from different sites in the same area and then examining their contents, the archaeologist is defining a *cultural unit*. In using his evidence in this manner, the archaeologist is applying one of the two principles of stratigraphy—the principle called the *law of strata identified by their contents*. This law, in a generalized form, states that depositional units, or associations, at different sites are contemporary with each other if they contain the same things in the same proportions.

Archaeologists not only discover the culture in a particular area at a given time; they also investigate how patterns changed through time and the step-by-step way in which one cultural unit was transformed into another. To do this, the archaeologist must first determine the sequence in which the cultural units occurred. Here he uses the other principle of stratigraphy, called the *law of superposition*, which states that the assemblage found at the bottom of a deposit is older than the ones above it in situations where mixing has not occurred, because it was laid down first.

Superposition of assemblages occurs in a variety of ways—a grave dug into old refuse, for example, or a house erected on the ruins of another building, or one layer of refuse dumped on top of another. Perhaps the most obvious case of superposition occurs where a site was briefly occupied, abandoned, and then reoccupied. Let us imagine, for a moment, a beach inhabited forty-five hundred years ago by a group of fishermen and shellfish collectors. Before they moved away, they littered the area with their garbage, some broken thorn fishhooks, bits of twined cotton cloth and nets, a few disc-shaped beads, and gourd containers. Windblown sand gradually covered the refuse and, a few hundred years later, another group of fishermen and shellfish collectors moved back to the same place. They too littered the area with garbage and left bits of woven cloth, broken shell fishhooks, and fragments of pottery with incised geometric designs scattered through their debris. The site was then abandoned, until an archaeologist came and excavated it. He first found the layer of refuse containing the pottery and other objects left by the later group; underneath was a layer of sand, and below the sand was the layer of refuse left by the first people. He could distinguish the two archaeological assemblages in his excavation by comparing the contents of the refuse layers. He could order them chronologically by the superposition of the strata in which they occurred.

The archaeologist suspected that human occupation might not have been continuous at the beach because of the sand layer and the differences between the two assemblages; however, he had no idea whether it took a day, a year, or a century for the sand layer to form. While looking for other signs of human occupation in the vicinity, he found and excavated another site. Here was only one layer, and it contained bits of twined cotton cloth, disc-shaped beads, pieces of stone bowls and undecorated pottery, and a few shell fishhooks interspersed among the food remains. What was the chronological relationship of this unit with the beach assemblages? Was it earlier than both, later than both, or intermediate in age? After comparing the contents of this assemblage with those from the beach, he decided it was intermediate in age—more recent than the lower unit at the beach and earlier than the upper one. It contained some objects—stone bowls and undecorated pottery—that occurred in neither of the beach assemblages, so he suspected its age to be slightly different from either of them. Still, it contained objects found in one or the other of the beach assemblages, suggesting that the three assemblages were fairly close to each other in time.

Seriation

In the example, the archaeologist used associations of contemporaneity to identify the two discrete beach assemblages, and stratigraphic evidence to place them in their correct chronological order. In addition, he used the technique of *seriation* to place the assemblage isolated at the other site between them. Seriation is based on the idea that assemblages which have many objects and associations in common are closer to each other in age than those which share only a few features or have nothing in common. The assumption underlying this idea is that cultural traits—like pottery, twined cotton cloth, or shell fishhooks—have continuous distributions in time under normal conditions, and, furthermore, that each trait has its own particular time span. Placing the isolated assemblage between those from the beach, rather than before or after them, does, in fact, give each trait a continuous time span, as Figure 1–1 shows.

The sequence that our archaeologist has established is a *relative cultural chronology.* It tells us that a particular assemblage is older than one assemblage and younger than another; it tells us the order in which things occurred. In some areas, where much archaeological research has been done, relative cultural chronologies spanning thirteen or fourteen thousand years and containing thirty or more clearly recognizable cultural units have been established on the basis of stratigraphic and seriational information. (See Chapter Three, pp. 52–63.) These long and

A RELATIVE CULTURAL CHRONOLOGY

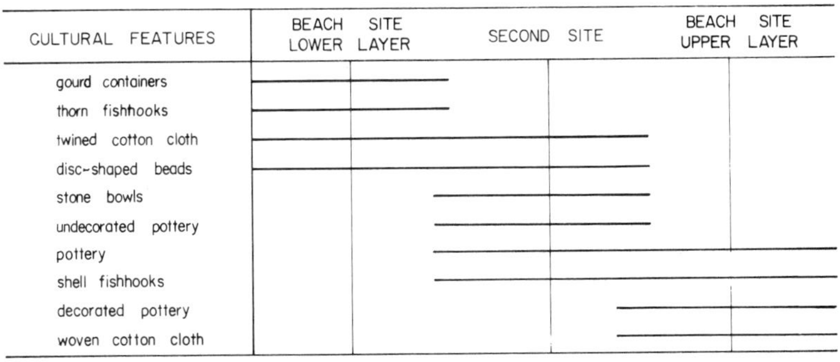

CULTURAL FEATURES	BEACH SITE LOWER LAYER		SECOND SITE		BEACH SITE UPPER LAYER	
gourd containers						
thorn fishhooks						
twined cotton cloth						
disc-shaped beads						
stone bowls						
undecorated pottery						
pottery						
shell fishhooks						
decorated pottery						
woven cotton cloth						

Fig. 1–1. The earliest cultural unit in the relative sequence is shown on the left side of the chart and the latest one on the right side. The horizontal lines indicate the time span of each cultural feature. By drawing vertical lines through the name of a particular cultural unit, it is possible to determine which features occur in that unit and which ones are diagnostic of it.

detailed cultural sequences allow the archaeologist to make precise interpretations and explanations of the processes of change in the area.

Usually, relative cultural chronologies are established in fairly small areas—such as an intermontane basin or a small river valley. In a large area, like Peru or Mexico, there are many of these localized relative chronologies. The many localized cultural chronologies within a single region reflect the cultural diversity of the New World. This diversity may range from slight differences in the ways that two potters decorate their products to broad, all-encompassing ones, such as the ways that different peoples gain their livelihoods or perceive the world around them. Further, this cultural diversity exists in both time and space: the farmers who lived in the pueblos of the American Southwest about A.D. 1000 lived differently from the peoples who inhabited the same area a thousand years earlier. These pueblo-dwelling farmers were also very different from their contemporaries to the northwest in the Great Basin who wandered from place to place throughout the year, collecting food in each locality as it became seasonally available.

Cross-dating

To understand local differences within a larger region, the archaeologist has to correlate the various local sequences with each other. Usually, he tries to determine which cultural units from different localities are contemporary with each other. By contemporary, he does not mean that the units have exactly the same age but merely that they can be assigned to the same period of time. The duration of these periods is highly variable: in some situations, thirty or forty years; in others, more than a millennium. Clearly, if the period is relatively short, the units assigned to it have a good chance of being nearly equal in age.

Cross-dating cultural sequences is a difficult but exceedingly important task. How it is done depends upon the kind of evidence that is available. Occasionally, cultural units in different regions are cross-dated on the basis of historical information or evidence obtained by some method of absolute dating—such as the radiocarbon technique. Sometimes they are cross-dated on the basis of geological evidence—such as when units in different localities were incorporated in the same widespread geological deposit. More commonly, however, they are cross-dated by some method that involves examining the objects and associations. One way this is done is to use trade goods, which are objects or associations that are common in one cultural unit and appear as intrusive elements in others. This technique was used to correlate several of the regional sequences in Mesoamerica during the first millennium A.D., when a kind of pottery manufactured in central Mexico was found associated with local ceramic styles near Guatemala City and in the Maya Lowlands. Another way to cross-date cultural units is to see whether they share a number of specific features—such as complex art styles or tool kits containing specific stone tools.

Absolute Dating

Another problem for the archaeologist is absolute dating. How old is a particular cultural unit? And how long did it last? To answer these questions, he relies on absolute dates expressed in years, decades, or centuries and usually correlated with the Christian calendar. Thus, when he says a particular cultural unit is 4500 years old—or 4500 B.P. (Before Present)—he is merely saying that it existed in 2500 B.C.

The absolute ages of cultural units can be determined in several ways. The simplest is when an object of known age appears in the cultural unit itself. In Peru, for example, blue glass beads were introduced by the Spaniards shortly after A.D. 1531. Thus, a cultural unit that contains blue glass beads can be no earlier than this date, although it may be somewhat later. Let us suppose that we found two superimposed assemblages in an excavation in Peru. The earlier one contained several blue glass beads, and the later one contained a decree written in Spanish dated 1571. The first unit, therefore, cannot be earlier than 1531 or later than 1571.

8   Unfortunately, we cannot date many New World cultural units

directly in terms of the Christian calendar because European goods did not begin to appear in the New World in any quantity until about 1500. This means that archaeologists working in the Americas have to rely largely on other methods of absolute dating and then correlate their results with the Christian calendar. A calendrical system was used by the Maya of southern Mexico and eastern Guatemala long before the Europeans came, and many cultural units in this area have been dated in terms of the Maya Long Count Calendar, so we know how long they lasted.[1] But we do not know how the Maya calendar correlates with the Christian calendar. Even the two most plausible correlations between the two calendrical systems differ from each other by slightly more than 256 years. In addition, the Maya calendar is of no use for dating cultural units outside of Mesoamerica, and is of little use for dating anything more than about three thousand years old.

Other widely used methods for determining absolute age in the New World are tree ring dating, or dendrochronology, and radiocarbon dating. Neither technique, however, gives exact dates, and the results of both have to be interpreted carefully. *Dendrochronology* is based on the assumption that each tree ring represents the growth that occurred in a single year. A master calendar, extending back to 53 B.C., has been built up in the American Southwest by matching variations in ring width on many specimens and counting back from one that was cut at a known time. When a specimen of unknown age is found, it can be dated by comparing its ring sequence with that of the master calendar.

There are several problems with tree ring dating. First, not every species of tree adds a growth ring each year. Some trees add them irregularly—two in one year and none the next—while others add them on only one side of their trunks. Trees of the same species, growing nearby but receiving slightly different amounts of sunlight and moisture, may add rings differently. Second, many of the sensitive species—like western yellow pine which is used for the master calendar in the Southwest—have relatively limited geographical distributions. The result is that there are several tree ring calendars—one for the area where western yellow pine grows and others for California or Georgia,

---

[1] When we write a date in terms of the Christian calendar—A.D. 1971, for example—we mean that one unit of a thousand years, nine units of a hundred years, seven units of ten years, and one unit of one year have passed since the birth of Christ. Maya Long Count dates are read in much the same way as our own, except that the basic unit in their calendar was the day rather than the year. Thus, a Maya Long Count date of 9.17.0.0.0 means that 9 units of 144,000 days, 17 units of 7200 days, 0 units of 360 days, 0 units of 20 days, and 0 units of 1 day have passed since the beginning point of their calendar. The Maya counted by eighteen instead of twenty in the third place of their calendar in order to make it approximate the length of the solar year.

where different species may be sensitive. Third, once a specimen—say, a house beam—is correlated with the master calendar, what does the resulting date actually tell us? Does it necessarily indicate that the house was built at the time the tree was cut? To answer that question, we must return to the archaeological evidence that is available.

Most of the absolute dates used in American archaeology result from radiocarbon age determinations. The *radiocarbon dating* method is based on the fact that a radioactive isotope of carbon—carbon 14 or C–14—produced in the upper atmosphere is eventually absorbed by every living thing on earth. Since living things are constantly absorbing and eliminating carbon compounds, each contains about the same proportion of C–14 as its environment and other living things around them. When an organism dies, it ceases to absorb carbon compounds, and the proportion of C–14 that it contains begins to diminish as the radioactive atoms disintegrate. By measuring the number of atoms that disintegrate during a known time, it is possible to compute the proportion of C–14 that is still present in the sample and, by comparing this with the proportion in living organisms, to compute its age. The next step, of course, is to determine the archaeological significance of the date that was obtained.

The radiocarbon dating technique also involves a number of assumptions, each of which is somewhat questionable. One is that the amount of C–14 produced in the atmosphere has been constant for a long time; and yet research during the past fifteen years has shown that this assumption is of limited validity. Hydrogen bomb explosions greatly increased the amount of C–14 in the atmosphere during the late 1950's and early 1960's, while the effect of using coal, petroleum, and other fuels that contain virtually no radioactive carbon because of their age was to diminish the proportion of C–14 in the atmosphere. Superimposed on these are also long-term variations in the rate of atmospheric C–14 production, probably caused by fluctuations in the activity of the sun. Whatever the causes of the variations, their effect is to distort the time scale defined by radiocarbon dates, as Figure 1–2 shows. Another assumption is that different environments—such as the atmosphere and a river flowing through an area with limestone bedrock—contain the same proportion of C–14. They do not. Living fish from aquatic environments where limestone is prevalent systematically yield radiocarbon ages of several hundred years, which suggests that the radiocarbon chronology for one kind of environment may be very different from one established for another. A third assumption is that different radiocarbon laboratories produce comparable results. This has been questioned by a few archaeologists

CALENDRICAL VS. RADIOCARBON AGES

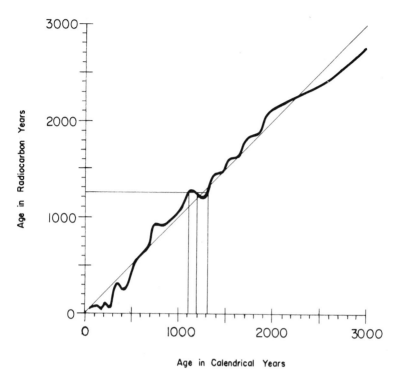

Fig. 1-2. Radiocarbon dates are expressed in the form of probability statements—for instance, 1250 ± 100 radiocarbon years B.P. (before the present, which is arbitrarily defined as A.D. 1950). In this example, 1250 is the mean, and the ± 100 indicates that there is a 67 percent probability that the actual age of the sample falls between 1150 and 1350 radiocarbon years or 100 radiocarbon years on either side of the mean value.

The correlation of radiocarbon ages with calendrical ages is complicated by a number of factors, one of which is short-term variations in the amount of radioactive carbon produced in the atmosphere. The effect of this variation is shown in the chart above: some radiocarbon dates—for example, 1250 radiocarbon years—may actually represent more than one calendrical date—1100, 1195, and 1325 in this particular instance. Hans Suess, *Journal of Geophysical Research* 70: 5950. 1965. American Geophysical Union, and Dr. Hans Suess.

but apparently not by many of the people who run radiocarbon laboratories. Despite the problems with absolute dating methods, archaeologists still must use them to develop an absolute chronology for the New World. But it is better to be aware of the limitations of the techniques than to accept and use their results indiscriminantly.

Conclusion

In one sense, there is very little to archaeology. The archaeologist has to deal with only two kinds of evidence—objects of all kinds and their associations with each other. In another sense, however, there is a great deal to archaeology, particularly when it comes to interpreting the meaning and significance of archaeological evidence. Much has been written about what the archaeologist can or cannot infer from his data; most of these limitations have been imposed either by people who are not archaeologists and consequently do not understand how to deal with archaeological evidence or by a few archaeologists who are either unwilling to concede or do not understand what they themselves are doing. What the archaeologist can and will learn about the past depends not only on the questions he asks when he collects his evidence but also on the kinds and numbers of questions he can ask about the meaning and implications of what he has found—not only the objects and associations themselves but also the larger patterns that exist among these data.

2. The Early Americans

For most of his last five million years, man lived exclusively in the Old World. No early forms of man—such as the australopithecines, *Homo erectus,* or *Homo sapiens neanderthalensis*—have ever been found in the New World, nor were there apes, either living or fossil, in the Americas. However, some time after he acquired his modern form (*Homo sapiens sapiens*) about fifty thousand years ago, man immigrated across the Bering Strait and settled for the first time in the Western Hemisphere. These immigrants from eastern Asia must have closely resembled the ancient inhabitants of that vast area. Today, the native peoples of the New World form a relatively homogeneous group characterized by several genetic traits either absent or exceedingly rare among Old World groups, including those of eastern Asia. Two examples of such genetic traits are the Diego Positive blood antigen, that is common among South American groups, and Carabelli's Cusp, an extra cusp on the inside of molar teeth, that is common in North America. These genetic differences, as well as those that exist among the American peoples themselves, are a result of evolutionary processes that began to operate when the first settlers arrived and continue to operate even now.

THE PLEISTOCENE WORLD

Man came to the New World during the later part of the Ice Age, or Pleistocene Epoch, which lasted from about three million to ten thousand years ago. The first thing that comes to mind about the Pleistocene Epoch is the periodic formation of ice sheets that grew to continental proportions in the upper northern latitudes, and mountain glaciers that grew to various sizes at high elevations in the temperate and tropical regions of the world. Other important changes also occurred during the glacial periods. The climates were different, the seas were lower, there were

13

different systems of lakes and rivers, and major natural environments—like tundra, temperate forest, or desert—were often far removed from their present locations. Glacial conditions usually prevailed for relatively brief intervals of time, separated from each other by long interglacial periods when moderate conditions, more or less resembling those of today, predominated.

American archaeologists are primarily concerned with the last glacial period—the Wisconsin Stage which began about seventy thousand years ago—and the succeeding postglacial period, because of man's relatively late arrival in the New World. Fortunately, we know more about these periods than the earlier Pleistocene Epoch, because their records have not been destroyed or obscured by later ice advances or the passage of time. It is clear that the world in which the first Americans and their descendants lived was very different from our own. To understand how the early Americans lived and why they lived where they did, we must understand what the Pleistocene world was like.

Climatic Variations

Many theories have been proposed to account for the periodic climatic and environmental changes that occurred during the Pleistocene. Variations in the amounts and kinds of solar energy reaching the earth were undoubtedly an important factor. The relationship between solar radiation and climate has been succinctly described by a meteorologist who said:

> Solar radiation supplies the energy, and the terrestrial atmospheric circulation is the mechanism of climate. . . . It is atmospheric circulation that produces weather and explains the distribution of such events as orographic rainfall, snow and snowfields, thermal instability, thunderstorms and tropical hurricanes, the extent of oceanic, continental, and arid climates.[1]

Changes in the kinds of solar radiation and their intensity produce changes in the world's climatic conditions by altering the patterns of atmospheric circulation. Over a period of time, these can produce changes in the size, shape, and location of major natural regions.

Paleobotanical, paleontological, and sedimentary evidence indicate that the climatic conditions at the height of the last glaciation differed in two ways from those that prevail today.

[1]H. H. Lamb, 1961, "Climatic Change Within Historical Times as Seen in the Circulation Maps and Diagrams," *Annals of the New York Academy of Sciences*, vol. 95, art. 1, p. 124.

First, there was an equatorward displacement and compression of all zonal wind systems resulting from the enormous expansion of polar circulation at the last glacial maximum. Second, the thermal equator—the line around the earth where the highest temperatures occur in a particular season—shifted a few degrees south of its present position, presumably because of the greater expansion of polar circulation in the Northern Hemisphere. These differences had many consequences.

A daily or seasonal weather pattern that is now typical in a particular place may have been unusual or absent there during the last glacial maximum. For example, the climate of the Chilean coast immediately south of Santiago is dominated by a dry, cool air mass in summer and by a moist, maritime air mass associated with westerly winds in winter. Consequently, summers are dry and winters are rainy in this area at the present time. During the last glacial maximum, however, the dry, cool air mass which is associated with a high-pressure cell located over the eastern Pacific Ocean was displaced northward toward the equator, and the dominant air mass throughout the year was the moist, maritime one; consequently, precipitation was abundant throughout the year instead of being seasonal, as it is now.

The differences between the modern and glacial climatic regimes affect the kinds of environments that occur in this area. The present climatic regime favors the development of scrub steppe—a community of plant species particularly well adapted to warm, dry summers and cool, wet winters. The regime at the time of the last glacial maximum led to the northward spread of temperate rain forest—a plant community that requires cool, wet conditions throughout the year—and its establishment in an area now covered with scrub steppe. The impact of climatic changes on the distribution of major natural regions in the New World can be seen clearly by comparing Figures 2–1 and 2–2.

The Wisconsin Stage

So far, we have said little about the last glacial period. When did it begin? What was it like?

The last glacial period is usually divided into three parts, each defined by a major event. During the Early Wisconsin Stage, from about 70,000 to 40,000 years ago, polar circulation was much more extensive than now, and glaciers covered much of Canada and the northern United States. The Middle Wisconsin Stage, from about 40,000 to 28,000 years ago, was a period when the atmospheric circulation system more or less resembled that of today, and the distribution of permanent ice sheets and glaciers may also have been similar. The Late Wisconsin Stage began about 28,000 years ago, when large ice sheets formed once again

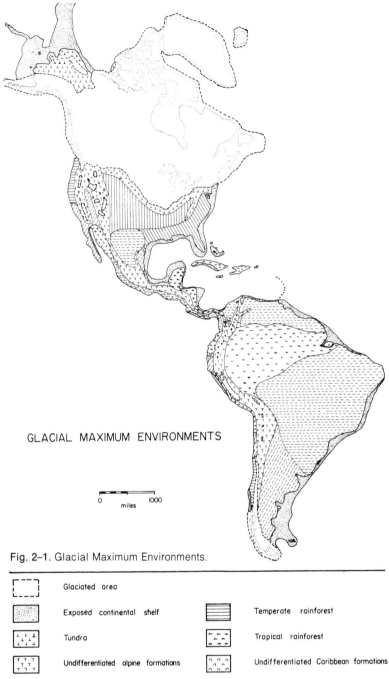

GLACIAL MAXIMUM ENVIRONMENTS

0 ____ 1000
miles

Fig. 2–1. Glacial Maximum Environments.

	Glaciated area			
	Exposed continental shelf			Temperate rainforest
	Tundra			Tropical rainforest
	Undifferentiated alpine formations			Undifferentiated Caribbean formations
	Temperate deciduous forest			Desert
	Coniferous forest			Scrub steppe
	Undifferentiated tropical deciduous forest & grassland			Undifferentiated prairie, grassland, scrub steppe & desert

MODERN ENVIRONMENTS

0   miles   1000

Fig. 2–2. Modern Environments.

Figs. 2–1 and 2–2. The distribution of major environmental zones is generalized in Figs. 2–1 and 2–2. The distribution of zones outside of the glaciated areas at the time of the last glacial maximum is very much generalized, and there are significant differences in the accuracy of various parts of this map. For example, we know relatively much more about the distribution of vegetation zones in the eastern United States or Alaska than we do about their distribution in Mexico, Central America, or the Amazon Basin.

in the Canadian highlands and slowly spread across the northern United States, reaching their maximum extent some ten thousand years later at about 16,000 B.C. Subsequently, the edge of the ice sheets retreated northward and their thickness diminished. Although the extent of the world's glaciers is constantly changing at the present time, something resembling the modern distribution of permanent ice probably existed about four or five thousand years ago.

The movement of the ice sheets during the Late Wisconsin Stage was anything but simple or continuous. It is difficult to describe these movements in a few words, but perhaps a good analogy is with the subtle patterns of moving water and wet sand that occur when waves wash over a beach as the tide comes in and recedes. In this analogy, the moving water corresponds to glacial ice, wet sand to formerly glaciated areas, high tide to the time of the glacial maximum, and the standing pools of water left after the tide recedes to remnants of glacial ice.

There were two centers of major continental glaciation in North America during the Late Wisconsin Stage. One was centered in the mountains of British Columbia and the other in the Laurentian Highlands of eastern Canada. The western ice sheet, called the Cordilleran Glacier Complex, was actually an interconnecting network of valley glaciers, mountain glaciers, and small ice sheets that stretched from the Columbia River Valley in the south to the Aleutian Islands in the north. The Laurentide Ice Sheet covered nearly five million square miles at the time of the last glacial maximum. It was more than eleven thousand feet thick near its center and several thousand feet thick near its edges. This ice sheet extended from the Ohio River Valley northward to the Arctic Ocean and from Newfoundland and the Atlantic Ocean to the eastern foothills of the Rocky Mountains in central and northern Alberta, where it merged in places with the Cordilleran ice mass.

Glaciation was much less extensive south of the Rio Grande River. There were small, isolated glaciers on the highest mountain peaks of Mexico, Central America, and the northwestern part of South America. In the mountains of central Peru—where permanent glaciers occur even today above sixteen thousand feet—there was a long continuous ice mass reaching down to about ten or eleven thousand feet at the time of the last glacial maximum. The plateaus of Bolivia, northern Chile, and northwestern Argentina were largely unglaciated because of the effects of dry cool air masses associated with high-pressure cells over the Atlantic and Pacific Oceans. Large glaciers reappeared in the Andes Mountains between Argentina and Chile near the 30th parallel and stretched southward in an unbroken chain to the southern end of the continent and Tierra del Fuego, where they spilled into both the Atlantic and Pacific Oceans. All of Chile, south of Chiloé Island, was covered with glacial ice, as was the Patagonian Plateau south of the Gallegos River.

Thousands of lakes were formed in both North and South America, as the glaciers advanced and retreated during the Late Wisconsin Stage. Some were formed by water melting from the glaciers themselves, while others were created by increased precipitation, ice dams, or the migration of subterranean water. Extensive systems of glacial and postglacial lakes existed in the Great Lakes region of North America and in the Great Basin of the western United States. Perhaps the largest of the glacial lakes in central North America was Lake Agassiz which covered much of southern Manitoba, Ontario, and northern Minnesota and, at its greatest extent, was larger than all of the Great Lakes combined. In the western United States, more than a hundred lakes formed in the Great Basin. The largest of these was Lake Bonneville which covered more than 20,000 square miles. The Great Salt Lake, one of Bonneville's descendants, is a mere puddle by comparison.

There were extensive lake systems in the plateaus and basins of central Mexico, and they were common on both sides of the Andes from Venezuela to the Straits of Magellan. Perhaps the most extensive development of lakes occurred in the plateaus of Bolivia and northern Chile, which in some ways are analogous to the Great Basin of the United States. Lake Minchín, the largest of the lakes in this region, covered nearly all of the central part of the Bolivian plateau and was many times larger than its modern remnant, Lake Poopo. Lake Ballivián was half again as large as its modern successor, Lake Titicaca, and was at least a hundred feet deeper.

Lower sea levels were another direct consequence of the last glaciation. The available evidence indicates that the seas stood near their present levels toward the end of the Middle Wisconsin Stage, roughly twenty-eight to thirty-five thousand years ago. However, as thousands of cubic miles of water became bound up in the great continental ice sheets of the Northern Hemisphere during the Late Wisconsin Stage, sea levels began to recede, slowly at first and then more rapidly as the thickness and extent of the ice masses increased. At the time of the glacial maximum, the sea level was slightly more than four hundred feet lower than it is now. As the glaciers diminished in size and thickness, the seas began to rise. This transgression was fairly rapid between fourteen and seven thousand years ago, and then it became more gradual as the seas approached their present level.

Large areas of the continental shelves of both North and South America were exposed because of the lower sea levels. The most extensive of these was probably the east coast of South America between Rio de Janeiro and Tierra del Fuego. The Falkland Islands which now lie more than four hundred miles from the mainland may well have been part of South America at the height of the Late Wisconsin glaciation. Other areas exposed by the lower sea levels include the northeastern coast of South America between Trinidad and the Bay of San Marcos in northern Brazil, the north coast of the Yucatán Peninsula, the west coast of Florida, a narrow strip along the eastern seaboard of the United States and Canada, and Beringia—the region between Alaska, Siberia, the Aleutian Islands, and the Arctic Ocean.

Lower sea levels had several other consequences on the environments of the Late Wisconsin Stage. Habitable coastal areas were much larger than they are now. Plant and animal communities that were characteristic of these regions during the last glacial period moved outward and became more extensive as the seas became lower. River gradients increased, and it is probable that some inland and coastal regions—such as the swampy Atrato River Basin between Colombia and Panama—were better drained than they are now. And, finally, the flow patterns of oceanic currents—like the Falkland Current that moves off the southeast coast of South America—may have changed significantly because of the different shapes of the continents, with important consequences to local environments.

Changes in Flora and Fauna

Paleobotanical and paleontological evidence dating from the Late Wisconsin Stage indicates at least three major effects of the changes in climate: one is in the size, shape, and configuration of plant formations; the second concerns shifts in the ranges of a number of animal species; and the third involves changes in the composition of the floral and faunal communities themselves, as some species became extinct and others appeared in the fossil record for the first time.

Many of the plant species survive today, although often in areas far removed from where their remains have been found. We frequently see a succession of plant formations in an area from late glacial times to the present. In southern New England, for example, which was completely covered with ice at the time of the last glacial maximum, tundra appeared shortly after the ice retreat. Spruce forest replaced the tundra vegetation as the ice receded even farther north, then pine forest, and finally a forest of hemlock and various deciduous trees. If we examine the present distribution of these plant formations, we find that tundra occurs largely in northern Quebec and Labrador, spruce forest in central Quebec and Labrador, pine forest immediately north of the St. Lawrence River, and mixed deciduous-coniferous forest in southern Quebec and New England.

By examining the climatic conditions of areas where certain plant formations occur today, we can make some rough calculations about the climatic conditions that prevailed in the areas where they grew in the past. In the preceding example, some of the tundra grasses and shrubs that grew in southern New England about 10,000 B.C. are the same ones that now grow in northern Quebec and Labrador. Consequently, the average summer and winter temperatures of northern Quebec at the present time may approximate those in the Boston area when tundra vegetation covered the ground and the edge of the Laurentide Ice Sheet, or large remnants of it, stood in the mountainous areas of southern New Hampshire, Vermont, and Maine. On the basis of this analogy, Boston may have had average January temperatures on the order of −25°F. and average July temperatures of about 50°F. at 10,000 B.C. Today, these months average 27°F. and 72°F., respectively, in the Boston area.

During late glacial times, many animal species also lived in localities well outside their present ranges. For example, there is a late glacial faunal assemblage in southwestern Kansas, dated about 9000 B.C., which contains a number of small mammals—masked shrews, water shrews, and meadow voles—whose present ranges do not extend this far south. The composition of the faunal assemblage suggests the fossil bed was formerly a marshy area surrounded by moist grassy meadow. We can also get some impression of the climate in this region near the end of the Pleistocene by observing present-day conditions where most of the fossil bed's species now live. This happens to be a part of South Dakota and Minnesota, where the precipitation is about 22 inches per year and the average temperatures are about 10°F. in January and 75°F. in July. These conditions probably resemble those in southwestern Kansas when the fossil bed was formed. Today, this part of Kansas receives about 20 to 25 inches of precipitation each year, and the average temperatures range from about 35°F. in January to about 80°F. in July.

Although animals disappeared from the fossil record throughout the Pleistocene Epoch, the best evidence for animal extinction in the Americas comes from the end of the period. A number of species—particularly large land mammals: the mammoth, mastodon, native American horse, giant bison, and ground sloth—became extinct after the last glacial maximum, when man was already present in the New World. The abundance of evidence from the late Pleistocene in comparison with the amount from earlier stages constitutes a sampling bias that makes it difficult to determine the relative importance of environmental changes, on the one hand, and man, on the other, as disturbing factors in the extinction process. All of the animals mentioned above have been found in association with cultural remains. Consequently, it is clear that man played a role in the disappearance of some species since the time of the last glacial maximum. The question that remains unanswered, however, is just how important his role was in the process as a whole.

The world of the Pleistocene was very different from ours. Moreover, in locating and using the resources they deemed necessary for life, the early Americans extracted energy from their natural environments and, by doing so, added to the changes that were already taking place. As these environments changed, so did the ways in which the early Americans defined their world.

THE FIRST AMERICANS ENTER ALASKA

Many archaeologists believe that neither land animals nor man could have entered the New World at times when Eurasia and North America were not connected by land, because the forty-mile stretch of water called the Bering Strait formed an effective barrier. There is some evidence, however, that it was not such a great barrier. First, at the Bering Strait, Siberia is visible from Alaska on clear days, and both mainlands can be seen from the Diomedes Islands which lie roughly midway between the two continents. This means that land would never be out of sight for anyone crossing, even if the sea level were as high as it is now. Second, caribou and fox—important food animals for the early inhabitants of the American Arctic—still move freely from Siberia and Alaska to the Diomedes Islands during the winter months when mushy ice covers the Bering Strait. Indeed, about once every ten years at the present time, the ice is firm enough for dog sled journeys from one continent to the other. Third, judging by the cultural similarities between Siberia and the American Arctic in postglacial times, the inhabitants of the two regions did exchange ideas and techniques even after the land bridge ceased to exist.

The Alaskan Environment

Judging by the evidence now available, the first immigrants entered the New World between twenty-five and thirty thousand years ago—at approximately the same time as, or slightly before, the Bering land bridge was beginning to emerge between North America and Siberia. Geological studies of the floors of the Bering and Chukchi Seas indicate that Beringia remained under water until the sea fell about 135 feet below its present level. At this time, small ribbons of land joined St. Lawrence Island to the two continental land masses. When the sea was over 400 feet lower than it is now, as it was during the last glacial maximum, the entire floor of the Chukchi Sea and the northeastern part of the Bering Sea platform were exposed, providing a land bridge from the Aleutian Islands in the south beyond the northern coast of Alaska and Siberia with an area of many thousand square miles. Streams flowed across the exposed land, and tundra and scattered patches of Arctic forest probably covered it. As the sea level rose after the glacial maximum, water finally covered the last remaining strip of land linking North America to Eurasia about 10,000 years ago.

When man first entered the perennially unglaciated area of central Alaska and the Yukon, he found it dissected by streams, dotted with small lakes, and covered with a variety of forest, grassland, and tundra environments that stretched for indeterminable distances eastward across northern Canada and southward through the intermontane valleys and basins of the Rocky Mountains. As the glaciers advanced, central Alaska and the Yukon probably became a refuge for both plants and animals particularly suited to its changing environment. The animals man encountered increasingly often—caribou, forest bison, steppe antelopes, musk-oxen, mountain sheep, mountain goats, fox, and beavers, to name only a few—were, by and large, the same ones he had known earlier in Siberia. At the same time, the American animals that had dwelled in this area when more moderate environmental conditions prevailed found it increasingly difficult to obtain their food and gradually moved southward into areas where such resources were becoming more plentiful.

The perennially unglaciated area of the American Arctic may have been more amenable to human occupation than either Siberia or Beringia, because its potentially usable resources were more varied and perhaps more plentiful than those of the areas to the east. The early inhabitants of central Alaska and the Yukon often camped in foothill country, where tundra or alpine grasslands covered the slopes of the ice-capped mountain ranges, and alders, birches, and willows grew around the lakes or streams on the valley floors. The foothill habitats have, on the whole, a much more diversified ecology than either the tundra or boreal forest environments, precisely because they usually occur along the boundaries or margins between these larger natural regions. For example, the foothill habitats are preferred by many of the Arctic animals and their predators, and the nature of the country provides many vantage points from which a hunting and gathering population could watch game trails. Thus, the plant and animal resources on which the early inhabitants of the American Arctic depended were certainly more varied and maybe more abundant in the foothill camping areas.

Population Movements

Man probably moved rapidly into the unglaciated area of the American Arctic and then into the semiglaciated intermontane and foothill areas to the east and south. He was spreading into major environmental regions that began in central Alaska and stretched for considerable distances in both directions. The resources he deemed necessary for life occurred throughout these regions, and he could live about as well in one part as in another.

During the year, these hunters and gatherers exploited some resources, particularly the plant foods, which were available only during certain seasons, and others, such as the caribou, which were available throughout the year. Some occurred only in special habitats, while others ranged more broadly. Consequently, each year a group would move through a number of food resource areas. In the long run, however, the resources available near the margins of these habitats changed as new climatic patterns emerged and perhaps as a result of limited overexploitation. Resources became scarcer along the northern and higher edges of the habitats as the climate became cooler, and eventually disappeared altogether. At the same time, they became more plentiful along the southern and lower edges of the habitats, and eventually spread into neighboring areas as favorable conditions appeared. Consequently, the ranges of the human populations changed as they followed the shifting location of their resources or encountered new ones when they moved into regions where different environmental conditions prevailed.

The groups that proceeded southward probably followed several different routes through Canada, depending to some extent on where the margins of the ice sheets were when they moved. Possibly some of them crossed into the Mackenzie Basin and moved southward along the eastern flanks of the Rocky Mountains, while others moved from central Alaska along the Pelly and Liard Rivers into the southern Yukon and northeastern British Columbia, following a route similar to the Alaskan Highway. It is difficult to determine, except in a general way, what routes these early populations could have taken, because we do not know the exact patterns of glaciation and their timing in western Canada. It is not clear, for example, whether the Laurentide Ice Sheet and the Cordilleran Glacier Complex merged along the entire eastern side of the Rocky Mountains in central and northern Alberta, forming a barrier, during the last glacial maximum or whether they coalesced in only a few widely separated localities.

When did human populations begin to move out of central Alaska and northern Canada? Let us review some of the pertinent evidence from both North and South America. Stone tools found in one of the lower levels of Wilson Butte Cave in southern Idaho were associated with organic materials that yielded a radiocarbon date of about 12,500 B.C. People lived, hunted, and left several different kinds of stone tool assemblages at various localities in the Valsequillo Reservoir of Puebla in south-central Mexico while the basin was filling up with eroded sediments between 16,000 and 6000 B.C. Finally, at Pikimachay Cave in the Peruvian highlands, near the modern city of Ayacucho, two stone tool assemblages were found in association with the remains of a variety of extinct animals. Radiocarbon dates on organic materials associated with the earlier assemblage range from 12,750 to about 20,000 B.C. A conservative estimate of its age would be between 13,000 and 14,500 B.C. The dates for the later assemblage average about 12,200 B.C.

In some ways, the relevant South American evidence is more abundant than that from North America. Many early sites have been found there. Stone tools from the El Abra rockshelter near Bogotá, Colombia are associated with radiocarbon dates that are slightly older than 10,000 B.C. Cut and burned bones, some of them from extinct animals, were found in the fossil-bearing localities at Muaco and Taima-Taima in north-central Venezuela; four radiocarbon dates from these sites—including some measurements on the cut and scored bones themselves—range from about 11,000 to 14,400 B.C. The stratified site of Cerro Chivateros on the central Peruvian coast has yielded three superimposed tool assemblages; radiocarbon dates place the end of the second cultural unit at about 8500 B.C. A nearby site, called Oquendo, has produced another tool complex that is intermediate in age between the first and second assemblage at Cerro Chivateros. Geological evidence suggests that the earliest assemblage at Cerro Chivateros—the Red Zone Complex—is slightly older than 10,000 B.C., while the Oquendo Complex is dated between 9000 and 10,000 B.C. Assemblages that are similar to these early stone tool complexes of the central Peruvian coast have also been found in coastal and highland Ecuador, northern Chile, northwestern Argentina, and northern Uruguay. Comparisons with the assemblages from the central coast of Peru and the later of the two assemblages from Pikimachay Cave—the Ayacucho Complex—suggest that some of them may be from the period between 10,000 and 12,000 B.C. That is, they are probably slightly older than the Red Zone Complex and not as old as the Ayacucho Complex. Finally, very different kinds of stone tools, associated with the remains of mylodon (a kind of giant ground sloth) and horse have been found in the lowest layer of Fell's Cave near the Strait of Magellan at the southern end of the continent. This layer has produced radiocarbon dates of 8770 and 9050 B.C.

The distribution of early stone tool assemblages in the New

Fig. 2-3. Early sites in the Americas, mentioned in the text.

World, as well as their antiquity, indicate that human populations were already living well south of the Canadian ice sheets at the time of the glacial maximum (16,000 B.C.) or even before. They were living in western South America at least by 14,000 B.C. and probably reached the continent several thousand years earlier. By 9000 B.C., they had already moved to the southern tip of South America. If men were already living in South America by 15,000 or 16,000 B.C., they must have been living in North America at an even earlier date. The implications are clear: human populations began moving southward out of the American Arctic before the last glacial maximum, and they spread throughout many, if not all, of the unglaciated portions of the New World before the end of the Pleistocene Epoch.

PLEISTOCENE TECHNOLOGY

This does not mean, of course, that man abandoned Alaska and northern Canada during the last glacial period, for there is ample evidence that the unglaciated portions of the American Arctic, which was merely an extension of Eurasia at that time, were more or less continuously occupied throughout the late Pleistocene. At the present time, we distinguish three broad groups of late Pleistocene tool assemblages in the American Arctic, on the basis of the stoneworking technology and tool types that predominate in each of them. These groups have different ages and geographical distributions. The two more recent ones may overlap somewhat in time but have been found in different parts of the American Arctic. Let us consider the content, antiquity, and relationships of these groups, beginning with the most recent one.

The most recent group, characterized by conical-shaped cores and by tools that were made on the blades and flakes removed

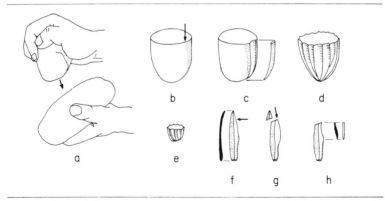

Fig. 2–4. The Conical Core Technique. *a*, A cobble of suitable chipping rock is split in half by direct percussion. *b*, A blow is delivered to the edge of the flat striking platform of the split cobble. *c*, This detaches the primary, or first, flake from the core. *d*, This illustrates the shape of the core after at least seventeen flakes have been removed in the same fashion. *e*, The core is expended when it is no longer possible or desirable to remove more flakes; the expended core is usually much smaller than it was when the primary flake was removed. *f*, The end of a flake opposite the original striking platform is detached as the initial step in making a burin, a tool with a chisel-shaped working edge that is used for cutting bone. *g*, The surface exposed in this step becomes the striking platform for detaching a second flake, or spall, in order to complete the manufacture of the burin. *h*, The finished burin.

from them, is found exclusively east of the Canadian Rockies. It contains two assemblages of pivotal importance for understanding the early history of man in the American Arctic. These are the Kluane Complex from the southwest Yukon and the Flint Creek Complex found at Engigstciak on the Firth River delta in the northwest Yukon. The importance of the Kluane materials is that they were buried in a soil zone that has been radiocarbon dated between about 8000 and 10,000 B.C. Since the tools cannot be younger than the soil in which they were incorporated (the tools were covered up as the soil was being formed), we can take these dates as indicative of the age of the Kluane Complex. This assemblage shares a number of specific features with the Flint Creek Complex, including bifacially chipped projectile points which link them with virtually all of the later tool assemblages in the American Arctic. The similarities between the two assemblages suggest that they probably have about the same age. The importance of the Flint Creek Complex, however, is that it was found overlying an earlier, very different kind of stone tool assemblage that has been called the British Mountain Complex. The cultural stratigraphy at Engigstciak, albeit badly disturbed by frost action in some parts of the site, gives us the chronological order of two of the groups.

The second group of assemblages has been found in central and northern Alaska, west of the Canadian Rockies. Consequently, its known geographical distribution is different from that of the group we have just discussed. Perhaps the most characteristic feature of the assemblages assigned to the second group is that they all contain wedge-shaped microcores and tools made on the blades that were removed from them. This stoneworking technique and also the shape of the cores themselves are very specific features that occur in a series of archaeological sites in northern Japan that date between about 12,000 and 8000 B.C. and in another series of sites in central Siberia that date from about 11,000 to 7000 B.C. None of the assemblages assigned to this group—either the Campus Site Complex or the Donnelly Ridge materials from central Alaska, to name only two—have been dated directly; however, because of their highly specific resemblances to certain materials in northern Japan and central Siberia, we can probably apply the radiocarbon measurements from northeast Asia with some confidence to date the Alaskan assemblages between about 10,000 and 8000 B.C.

There is one assemblage, called the Akmak Complex, from the lowest levels of Onion Portage on the banks of the Kobuk River in northwestern Alaska that is virtually unique among the stone tool complexes of the American Arctic at the present time. This is undoubtedly due to the small amount of archaeological research that has been carried out in this vast area. The Akmak Complex

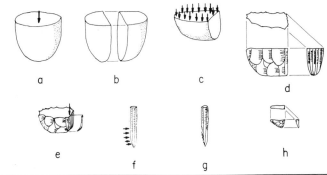

Fig. 2–5. The Microcore Technique. *a*, A split cobble of suitable chipping rock is quartered by direct percussion. *b*, The two unused cores. *c*, Multiple blows are delivered to the flat striking platform of the core in order to trim or prepare it for the removal of microblades. *d*, Top, side, and front views of the prepared microcore. *e*, Microblades are removed from the front end of the core by direct percussion flaking. *f*, Chips are removed from one side of a microblade. *g*, The partially backed blade produced by removing chips from the edge of the blade. *h*, The expended microcore is much smaller than the core blank and may have a very different shape. A microcore is a core that is prepared in such a way that a lot of small blades can be removed from it. The blades are then made into tools. The advantage of the microcores over many other kinds of cores is that they are very economical, in that very little raw material is wasted. Some of the other core preparation techniques—e.g., the Levallois technique shown in figure 2–6—are quite wasteful since only one or two of the flakes removed are actually made into tools. Literally dozens of tools can be made from the blades removed from a microcore of roughly the same size as the Levallois core.

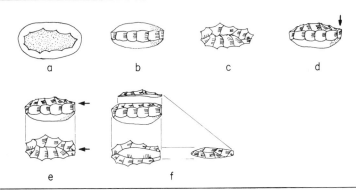

Fig. 2–6. The Discoidal or Prepared Core Technique. *a*, The sides of a cobble are trimmed by direct percussion flaking. *b*, Side view of the partially trimmed core. *c*, The top is now trimmed. *d*, A striking platform is prepared at one end of the core by a combination of percussion flaking and grinding. *e*, The prepared flake is removed from the top of the core by percussion flaking directed at the striking platform. *f*, Top and side views of the prepared core and the flake that was removed from it. The kind of prepared core technique shown in this illustration is also called the Levallois technique.

contains a few microcores; however, they are somewhat different from those found in the microcore assemblages mentioned above. Akmak also contains some disc-shaped bifaces that occur in central Siberian assemblages that have been radiocarbon dated between about 13,000 and 10,000 B.C. and in some of the assemblages that can be assigned to the third group, which we will consider below. In many ways, the Akmak Complex is intermediate between the second and third group of assemblages, and the presence of microcores in it suggests that the microcore technique of stoneworking is probably somewhat older in the American Arctic than the conical-core technique. Judging by their relationships with other assemblages, the Akmak materials probably date somewhere between about 12,000 and 10,000 B.C.

The oldest group contains at least half a dozen assemblages, found on the Arctic slopes of the Brooks Range in northern Alaska and Canada and at Fisherman Lake in the southwest corner of the Northwest Territories. These assemblages are poorly known for the most part, but all of them contain tools with steeply retouched edges that were made on flakes or blades with prepared striking platforms that were removed from discoidal cores. This technique of stoneworking consists of chipping the surface of a suitable rock or cobble in such a way that the shape of the few flakes or blades that can be removed from it are predetermined before they are detached.

There are several independent lines of evidence indicating that the assemblages assigned to this group are the oldest now known in the American Arctic and that they probably span a considerable period of time. Perhaps the weakest comes from the disturbed lower layers at Engigstciak, where tools of the British Mountain Complex were found at the same depth as pollen and animal remains which suggest that the climatic conditions at that time were at least as warm as those of today, if not warmer; the last time that such conditions could have prevailed was well before the last glacial advance in Canada, perhaps toward the end of the Middle Wisconsin Stage. The second line of evidence is provided by the geological context in which the McLeod Complex was found near Fisherman Lake. This assemblage was incorporated in a soil zone that formed after 30,750 B.C., either about 21,000 or 16,000 B.C., depending on how the geological history of this region is interpreted. The third line of evidence is based on comparisons with Upper Palaeolithic cultures in northeast Asia. The stone tool assemblages in this group have their greatest similarities with the Mal'ta, Buret', and Irkutsk Military Hospital complexes of central Siberia, all of which are dated about 28,000 B.C. on the basis of the geological contexts in which they occur, and with the main cultural horizon at Afontova Gora II which has been radiocarbon dated at 18,950 B.C. The American

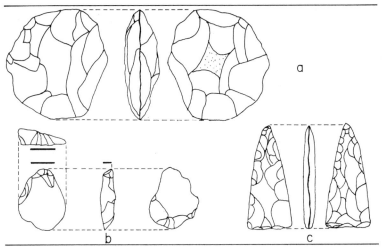

Fig. 2-7. Chipped stone tools. *a*, Disc-shaped biface similar to those found in the Akmak Complex. *b*, Steeply retouched scraper, the scraping edge of the implement demarcated by the heavy line. *c*, Bifacially chipped projectile point.

Arctic assemblages share fewer features with central Siberian cultures that are older than Mal'ta or more recent than Afontova Gora II. This may be somewhat fortuitous, however, because the earlier assemblages in that region probably date before 70,000 B.C., while the later are certainly no older than about 13,000 B.C. This means that the Mal'ta, Buret', and Irkutsk Military Hospital assemblages, on the one hand, and the Afontova Gora II assemblage, on the other, are isolated in time, not only from each other

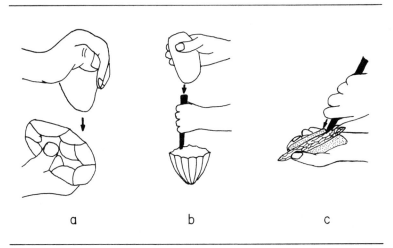

Fig. 2-8. Stone Chipping Techniques. *a*, Direct percussion flaking. *b*, Indirect percussion flaking or the punch technique. *c*, Pressure flaking.

but also from the materials that precede and follow them. Unfortunately, the gaps in the cultural sequence of central Siberia occur exactly during the period that is of most interest for comparative purposes. We can, however, remedy this deficiency a little by comparing the early American assemblages with ones from northern Japan that date between 18,000 and 13,000 B.C. These assemblages—mainly from the vicinity of Shirataki on Hokkaïdo Island—are not well known at the present time; in spite of this, it is clear that they do not closely resemble the early group of stone tool complexes in the American Arctic. Although the evidence is weak, it can be interpreted as indicating that the early group of assemblages in the American Arctic dates from between about 23,000 and 12,000 B.C.

The discoidal core and edge-retouch technology that characterizes this group also occurs in other early stone tool assemblages in the New World. The steeply retouched scraper from Friesenhahn Cave in eastern Texas, that was apparently associated with a number of extinct mammalian species, could well have been made by this technique. The discoidal core and edge-retouch technology also occurs in the early assemblages at Valsequillo, Mexico and in those of western South America between Ecuador and northern Chile. We have already indicated that the earliest known of the South American assemblages—the Paccaicasa and Ayacucho Complexes from Pikimachay Cave—are older than 12,000 B.C., while some of the later ones containing edge-retouched tools—the Red Zone, Oquendo, and Exacto Complexes—are all earlier than 9000 B.C.

There seems to have been an early, very widespread technological horizon in the New World that lasted from about 23,000 to 12,000 B.C. Unfortunately, we know relatively little about the assemblages that belong to this period; most of them have been discovered only during the last decade and only a few have been studied adequately. We can recognize chronological differences between these assemblages only in localities—like Fisherman Lake, Ayacucho, or the central Peruvian coast—where more than one of them has been found. Undoubtedly, further research will add a great deal to our understanding of what happened during this period and how these early peoples lived. At the present time, however, we can only say with certainty that extinct animals were killed and presumably eaten at some sites—like Valsequillo or Pikimachay Cave—and that marine shellfish were eaten at another site located on the Peruvian coast.

We can, however, speculate a little about the significance of this widespread technological horizon. The similarities between the early assemblages in the Americas and northeast Asia suggest that the first inhabitants of the New World brought the discoidal core and edge-retouch technology with them when they emigrated and that they carried these techniques with them as they moved out of the American Arctic before the last glacial maximum. The spread of this technology may well be related to the spread of the first human populations throughout the unglaciated areas of the New World.

Demographic Changes and Environmental Diversity

We should probably view the spread of man throughout the New World in terms of a model that emphasizes environmental change and population growth rather than deliberate, long-distance migration. Such a pattern of spread and settlement would resemble a slowly moving wave, originally expanding southward from Alaska and northern Canada and then from secondary centers located south of the Canadian ice sheets. This view implies that population growth was substantial during the later part of the Pleistocene Epoch, as groups continually moved into previously unoccupied areas and began to exploit their resources. It also implies that cultural diversity developed, as populations adapted their behavior to the particular environmental conditions that prevailed in different areas.

We have already emphasized the environmental changes that took place in the late glacial period. The size, shape, and location of both the major natural regions and the habitats that compose them changed, as did the availability and abundance of their resources. Now let us consider the accompanying demographic changes that may also have occurred. As human populations moved into previously uninhabited resource areas, their size increased—perhaps sometimes nearly doubling each generation—because of the abundance of resources that had not been used earlier. Some of the resources they used undoubtedly replenished themselves each year; others probably did not. If the size of the population were to expand indefinitely—beyond the culturally defined carrying capacity of the resource areas that were being exploited—then the per capita food available would begin to diminish as long as its economic orientation remained the same.

As a population became too large to feed itself adequately, the group divided. The larger remnant probably stayed behind, at a level where the available food now became sufficient to feed everyone. The smaller part of the group—probably one or at most a few families—moved out and colonized a nearby set of uninhabited resource areas.

The size at which this division occurred must have varied considerably, depending on several factors. One was obviously the availability and abundance of the culturally defined resources. These resources consisted not only of food and water, but also of fuel, shelter, and materials for making tools. If the resources were readily available and plentiful, then the area could support a larger population. Another factor determining the size of a population was its economic orientation. A seacoast, for example, might have provided a relatively inhospitable habitat for a group that did not exploit marine resources; consequently, that group might be smaller than another group occupying a similar habitat and utilizing the abundant resources of the sea.

As human populations spread from one natural region to the next in the New World, they continually had to cope with environmental diversity. The natural resources of new habitats were likely to be partly or completely different from old ones. First, they had to recognize that some of the natural products of the new area were potentially important resources; then they had to decide to exploit these resources at the expense of other ones; and finally, they often had to modify old techniques of exploitation or devise new ones in order to use the new resources. The cultural expression of environmental differences—differences not only in the availability of certain resources but also in their seasonality—was that the patterns of work, as well as the timing of certain activities, varied considerably from one group to another.

This kind of cultural variation was not limited entirely to groups that lived in different natural regions. It undoubtedly occurred also among groups that had different territories within the same natural region. One thing that is clear from many ecological studies is that plants and animals—potential food resources—are neither uniformly nor randomly distributed throughout a major natural region. They cluster or concentrate in certain places where the resources they need for life are available. As a result, any natural region is a mosaic composed of many different habitats, or from a human perspective, resource areas. What was an important resource for one population may have been unimportant to the neighboring group. Consequently, the intensity, duration, and scheduling of their work activities may have been significantly different.

The evidence we have indicates that there was, in fact, this kind of diversity among the economic orientations of the various groups living in the New World before 12,000 B.C. The land animals used at Valsequillo, Engigstciak, or Pikimachay Cave not only differed from each other but also stand in marked contrast with the marine shellfish that were used at Tortuga on the central Peruvian coast. The differences among the faunal remains at these sites suggest that food resources were defined differently at each and that different techniques of food procurement were practiced. In effect, all we are saying is that there was economic and presumably cultural variation among the earliest hunting and gathering groups in the New World, in spite of the fact that they were making and using essentially the same kinds of stone tools throughout this vast area. Furthermore, the diversity increased with the passage of time, as groups continued to redefine the resources of their territories and to accommodate themselves to the new and still emerging situations.

Late Pleistocene Cultural Diversity

Cultural differences among groups, barely perceptible previously, become obvious during the later Pleistocene—from about 14,000 to 9000 years ago. There are at least thirty or forty times as many sites known from late glacial times as from the preceding period. There is also much greater variation in the kinds of stone tool assemblages they contain.

In one sense, some of the differences we perceive between the two periods may be more apparent than real because of patterns of archaeological exploration, which have produced a very peculiar distribution of sites in both time and space. In North America, there are very few sites known that have occupation layers dating between 12,000 and 10,000 B.C., while there is a fairly large number of sites known with occupations dating between 10,000 and 7000 B.C. This means that we have a blank spot in the archaeological record of North America that spans at least two millennia and separates the earlier discoidal core and edge-retouch assemblages from the later, well-studied ones. The situation is somewhat different in South America, where there is no appreciable gap in the archaeological record between 12,000 and 7000 B.C.; however, none of the South American assemblages dating from this period have been studied as thoroughly as some of the early complexes to the north.

Nevertheless, the differences between the two periods are significant. There are many late Pleistocene archaeological sites, including very specialized ones, such as places where animals were killed and butchered or workshops where stone tools were made. These have been found in many of the unglaciated portions of the New World. Even where few sites or none have been found, there are often isolated finds of artifacts identical to those found in late glacial assemblages elsewhere. An excellent example of this is the many stray Clovis projectile points found in areas drained by the Tennessee and Ohio Rivers. Projectile points with the same form have been found in archaeological contexts in New Mexico and Nova Scotia yielding radiocarbon dates of about 9500 and 8600 B.C. These isolated finds indicate, minimally, that populations were moving through these areas before the end of the Pleistocene Epoch. The relative abundance of materials dating to late glacial times—whether well-defined archaeological sites or isolated surface specimens—implies that the total population of the New World was substantially greater than it had been earlier. Population growth was probably continuous from the time men first entered the New World and began to fill up previously unoccupied areas; however, the growth rate may not have been uniform in all regions for some have a greater variety and abundance of resources than others. This population increase becomes first really apparent only toward the end of the Pleistocene.

As to increased cultural variation—not only in the kinds of economic orientations seen in the archaeological remains but also in the kinds of stone tools made and used by different populations—the amount of diversity among late Pleistocene archaeological assemblages appears much greater than during the preceding period, and it appears to have increased more or less continuously with the passage of time. This process of divergence or regionalization becomes very apparent in the archaeological record from about 10,000 to 7000 B.C. By this time, the discoidal core and edge-retouch stoneworking technology that had been so widespread earlier was either modified into or replaced by a series of contemporary, regional stoneworking traditions that had limited geographical distributions.

Before considering the significance of this process of diversification, let us briefly examine the different regional stoneworking traditions that existed in the New World toward the end of the Pleistocene Epoch. We have already mentioned two of them—the Alaskan microcore tradition and the Yukon conical core tradition. The others are the fluted projectile point, the stemmed projectile point, and the leaf-shaped projectile point traditions in North America and the Andean biface tradition in western South America.

The most widespread of the North American traditions is characterized by a variety of projectile points with fluted surfaces or thinned basal edges. These are associated in a number of localities with a wide range of tools that were made on flakes and blades. Assemblages containing these materials, as well as an enormous number of isolated surface finds, occur from Nova Scotia to California and from southern Canada to northern Mexico. This tradition dates between about 9500 and 7000 B.C. and can be subdivided into three chronologically distinct stages, each of which is characterized by a particular technique of preparing the basal portion of the projectile point for removing the channel flakes that produce the fluted or thinned surfaces.

The early stage of the tradition, which dates from about 9500 to 9000 B.C., is characterized by a single widespread kind of projectile point and technique for finishing them. The assemblages contain Clovis points, and the fluted surfaces were produced by striking relatively long, narrow channel flakes from a basal platform that was roughly symmetrical in cross section and not elaborately prepared. We can call this the Llano technique, since most of the Clovis points made in this way come from a small number of assemblages that are referred to as the Llano Complex. These assemblages were found at sites where mammoths were killed and butchered on the high plains of Oklahoma, Colorado, New Mexico, and southern Arizona. The only assemblage east of the Mississippi River that contains Clovis points made with the Llano technique is from the Shoop site in southeastern Pennsylvania. Besides the Clovis points found in these assemblages, many isolated finds have been made throughout the United States; however, it is not clear whether they belong to this stage or to the succeeding one, because the technique of manufacture is usually not specified in their descriptions.

The middle stage of the tradition dates from about 9000 to 8000 B.C. It is characterized by fluted points that were made by a technique involving elaborate preparation of the basal edge before the channel flakes were removed. The technique involves beveling the base of the point and making a wavy striking platform with small protuberances that served as guides for removing the channel flakes. There was more diversity in the kinds of projectile points that were made during this stage than in the preceding one; however, the other tools found in the assemblages tend to be fairly similar over vast areas. Assemblages on the western plains from Montana to Texas contain Folsom projectile points, as well as unfluted forms. These assemblages are usually called the Folsom Complex and are often associated with the remains of extinct bison. Assemblages east of the Mississippi River contain Clovis points and have been referred to as the Eastern Clovis Complex. The eastern populations may have hunted mastodons in the forests around the Great Lakes and probably relied intensively on small herd animals, like caribou, in the Northeast.

The late stage in the tradition dates from about 8000 to 7000 B.C. and is characterized by considerable regional variation in the kinds of projectile points that were made and used. The great range of fluted or basally thinned points in the eastern United States that belong to this stage are probably local developments out of the earlier and more widespread Eastern Clovis Complex. In the high plains, the Folsom Complex was replaced by a series of regional complexes with more limited geographical distributions. Each of these seems to contain a particular kind of basally thinned projectile point, and many of them are associated with bison remains.

A tradition of bifacially chipped projectile points with long stems apparently emerged in the Columbia Plateau—southern Idaho, eastern Oregon, and eastern Washington—between 11,000 and 10,000 B.C., persisting until about 6000 B.C. This tradition, or a closely related one with large stemmed points, probably predominated in the Great Basin and California as well during the period between 8000 and 5000 B.C., although the evidence is not yet as conclusive as it might be. The shape of the stemmed points in this area not only changed with the passage of time but probably also varied somewhat from one locality to another, particularly during the later part of the period. Faunal remains associated with assemblages containing stemmed points indicate that the economic orientations of different populations ranged from the use of riverine resources at the Five Mile Rapids site in eastern Oregon to the exploitation of plant foods and land mammals—such as deer, fox, muskrat, and rabbit—at the Lind Coulee site.

The last North American tradition is composed of assemblages that contain leaf-shaped Lerma projectile points. These are made almost exclusively by percussion flaking and are associated with a small range of other stone tools. The tradition probably dates between about 8000 and 7000 B.C. and is known mainly from northern and central Mexico. The populations that made Lerma points subsisted on a variety of wild plants and on animals that they hunted or trapped. Different kinds of faunal remains are associated with the various assemblages of this tradition. Populations in the Valley of Mexico occasionally hunted mammoths, while those in the mountains of northeastern Mexico hunted deer and beaver. To the south, the inhabitants of the Tehuacán Valley hunted deer and antelope and trapped small animals—like rabbits, gophers, and rats.

Another widespread stoneworking tradition occurs in western South America from Venezuela in the north to Argentina and Chile in the south. It has been called the Andean Biface Horizon and probably dates between 12,000 and 7000 B.C. The early assemblages of the tradition are fairly uniform over a vast area and typically contain large percussion-flaked bifaces, spear points, denticulates, and flake scrapers. By about 8000 B.C., there was considerable regional variation in the kinds of stone tools made in western South America. At least three regional traditions or groups of assemblages are derived from the earlier widespread group. The Venezuelan assemblages that probably date between 8000 and 7000 B.C.—like El Jobo and Cucuruchú—are distinguished from those to the south by their pressure-flaked projectile points and large keeled scrapers. The central Peruvian assemblages retained virtually all of the kinds of implements that occurred in the earlier assemblages and merely added several kinds of small, percussion-flaked points to the tool kit. The populations of northern Chile and the plateaus of northwestern Argentina began to make their tools on large punch-struck blades. The only firm evidence we have about the subsistence activities of these populations is that the inhabitants of Cucuruchú occasionally hunted small mastodons, ground sloths, and glyptodonts. The environmental situations that prevailed in the other regions, where these assemblages occur, suggest that their inhabitants relied on very different sets of food resources—perhaps shellfish on the Peruvian coast and herds of camelids in northern Chile and northwestern Argentina.

Conclusion: The Process of Diversification

All these variations among archaeological assemblages dating from late glacial times reflect a process of divergence which must have begun when the first immigrants arrived in the Western Hemisphere and which was the product of several interrelated factors, population growth and environmental change being two of the more obvious. As the total New World population increased, the number of bands of people probably increased also, which would have had several consequences. First, there was probably increasing territoriality as New World resource areas were gradually filled. This situation would have favored the development of more specialized tools and techniques for extracting the resources in each particular territory. Second, there would have been increasing isolation between the various bands. Groups were undoubtedly aware of what their immediate neighbors were doing, but probably less familiar with what was happening three or four hundred miles away, even though there is evidence that exchange networks occasionally operated over these distances. They were probably completely unaware of what was happening in very distant localities.

Some of the cultural variation that existed during the late Pleistocene was undoubtedly the product of personal or group preferences; however, alterations of the environment can also produce cultural variation. As the ranges of various plants and animals gradually shifted in response to the climatic changes that took place in late glacial times, the old food resources of certain areas were replaced by new ones. These changes would be most apparent in areas located near the boundaries between major natural regions—such as grasslands and forests. In the Tehuacán Valley, for instance, the inhabitants began to rely increasingly on white-tailed deer and cottontail rabbits toward the end of the Pleistocene. The animals they hunted earlier—pronghorn antelope and jack rabbits, to name only two—moved northward to areas where more favorable habitats occurred. The faunal shift in Tehuacán was probably not apparent to the north where the amount of environmental change may have been less. In Tehuacán, the shift was accompanied by a change in hunting techniques that reflected the behavioral patterns of the new animals. To the north, groups presumably continued to hunt antelope and jack rabbits in the same ways that their ancestors had. Thus, a pattern of exploitation that was once uniform over a large area persisted in one part of it and was replaced in the other by a different pattern as new resources became available.

Throughout the chapter, we have alluded to the relationship between population size and resource exploitation. Although in the simplest terms, the economic orientation of a population sets the upper limits on its size, there are many interrelated factors that make up a group's economic orientation. For example, in any region, a population must first define what elements of its natural environment will constitute resources and then determine their abundance and productivity. These elements only become productive resources when the group has the means—the knowledge, tools, and techniques—for using them. In this way, the population itself is defining the carrying capacity of its environment and is ultimately setting the limits on its size.

Populations not only define the resources of their environments but also what they need from them through their habits of resource consumption, or standards of living. Let us assume, for the moment, that two populations are exploiting two identical food resources of the same size. One group has a 3000 calorie daily diet and the other has a 1500 calorie daily diet. The relationship between population size and resource consumption is clear in this situation. If the groups have the same size, then the second one can sustain itself for twice as long as the first on the same amount of food, or, if the second population is twice as large as the first, then it can sustain itself for the same length of time.

Other factors are also involved in this relationship—for instance, the extent of the group's territory, trade, wastage, or the intensity of resource utilization, to name only a few. Many of these factors are not independent of each other, for they interact in exceedingly complex ways. The extent of resource utilization may reflect population size or consumption habits as much as it determines them. Consequently, population size is not the dependent variable in this relationship. It is merely another one of the factors involved in a system where a change in one factor will ultimately lead to changes in the others. At one point in the history of a group, population size may be the most important of the factors producing change; at another time, it may be a relatively unimportant one, responding to changes among the other factors rather than producing them.

3. The Emergence of Food Production

The economic orientations that were emerging in the New World toward the end of the Pleistocene Epoch were highly differentiated ones, in the sense that they usually consisted of more than one method of acquiring food and exploiting other resources. In the Tehuacán Valley, for example, the varying sizes of contemporary archaeological sites, their locations in different ecological zones, and the different kinds of food remains found in each indicate that the population harvested a series of wild plants that ripened at slightly different times during the late spring, summer, and early fall. This produce was supplemented with small game—such as rabbits and gophers—that could be trapped in the immediate vicinity of the camp. When the plant foods were nearly exhausted in the late fall, the group divided into several small bands that moved into different parts of the valley, where they turned to hunting deer and to collecting certain wild plants available throughout the year. Once the prickly pears and cactus ripened again in the spring, the bands came together in order to harvest them.

Thus, the food acquisition activities performed by the members of a group intermeshed with each other in various ways, depending on the resources being used, their seasonal availability, and their relative importance in the diet. These activities define an important part of the economic orientation of a group. These orientations could vary considerably between groups—even ones living in the same natural region—because of local differences in the availability of resources or different valuations placed on particular resources. For example, there were two contemporary populations living about ten miles from each other in the coastal desert of central Peru—one near a sandy beach and the other near a rocky point. Virtually all of the shellfish consumed by the first group were beach-dwelling species, and virtually all of the shellfish consumed by the second group were rock-dwelling species.

The diversity between groups is often underemphasized by the names applied to their economic arrangements. Frequently, one method of food acquisition—such as line fishing in rivers—is selected and used to characterize the entire economic system. Yet, though fishing may indeed have been an important activity throughout the year, it may also have been carried on for only a few weeks and thus have been relatively unimportant in terms of the whole year. By calling a group a fishing society, we obscure the fact that its members exploited other resources. When we call two different groups fishing societies, we imply that they may have shared one method of resource exploitation, which is not necessarily so because fishing can be done in a variety of ways. By comparing the two societies in this manner, we also obscure the facts that fishing may have occupied a very different place in the two economies and that their other economic activities may have been very different. The importance of this diversity is that it provided a pool from which further adaptations to the environment were derived.

The variety of economic orientations we can recognize in the archaeological record appears to increase after the end of the Pleistocene Epoch. By 6000 B.C., the inhabitants of the central Peruvian coast were intensively exploiting the resources of vegetated areas located in the fog belt in winter and the wild plant and animal resources found in the river valleys in summer. Groups in the Great Basin began to rely for increasingly long periods each year on the food resources of rivers and old glacial lakes. Some populations in the San Francisco Bay region of California abandoned the littoral harvesting activities of their ancestors and turned to the acorns and other plant foods that grew in the interior. Peoples living along the rivers of Kentucky, Tennessee, and Alabama about 5000 B.C. began to exploit freshwater mussels as a permanent food source, supplementing them with the wild plants and small game that abounded in the nearby forests. These examples reflect a continuation of the process of cultural diversification, mentioned in the last chapter, that began when men first entered the New World.

In the simplest terms, the cultural diversity that was appearing in the New World after the end of the Pleistocene was produced by the isolation of groups from each other and by their increasingly efficient adaptation to the environments in which they lived. The picture we have for this period, however, is anything but simple, because different populations adapted to their environments in various ways at different times. For example, the littoral harvesting activities that were emerging along the Peruvian coast were similar in many ways to the littoral harvesting techniques that were gradually being abandoned around San Francisco Bay. Furthermore, different groups living in the same environmental setting often defined and used its natural resources very differently. The Saginaw Valley of Michigan, for instance, was occupied by three distinct groups in historic times. The Ottawa and the Huron hunted and fished in the valley during the summers and left it during the winters, while the Potawatomi farmed its land in the summer and hunted its small game animals in the winter.

Economic patterns in a few regions—like the heavy reliance on forest products in the eastern United States—were remarkably stable and changed very little once they became established. In some areas—like the Tehuacán Valley—there was a succession of different economic orientations, each evolving slowly from the preceding. In other areas——like the central coast of Peru—there were occasionally radical economic changes that lacked local archaeological antecedents and represent outside influences. We can view what happened in each area as a line of economic development. Occasionally, a line was relatively uniform in an area, and all of the resident populations participated in it; at other times, neither was the case. More important, however, is the fact that there were many lines of economic development in the Americas.

This chapter is focused on a particular kind of economic orientation that emerged independently and probably in various ways in different parts of the New World: agriculture. Most generally, agriculture means producing one's food rather than collecting it. Many different kinds of agriculture were practiced in the New World and were integrated into economic systems in a variety of ways. Some agricultural systems, like multi-crop irrigation farming, are labor intensive and require large inputs of both time and energy. Other agricultural systems—such as single-crop river bank, or floodwater, farming—are not particularly labor intensive and do not require much time or energy. The net result is a great deal of variation among agrarian societies.

Despite the widespread practice of agriculture throughout much of the New World, it was not necessarily the most important economic activity in all agrarian societies. Several groups in the Amazonian lowlands of South America supplemented the wild foods they obtained from the rivers and forests with agricultural produce that they grew occasionally or even collected from old, abandoned fields. Other populations—like the buffalo hunters of the Great Plains—even abandoned the food-producing activities of their ancestors, because alternative economic orientations were either more advantageous or more appropriate under the particular social conditions that prevailed.

In addition, agrarian economies were not necessarily more

productive than other economies. Some populations that did not practice agriculture—for instance, the littoral harvesters of the Northwest Coast—spent very little time and energy collecting the resources they needed and even occasionally amassed considerable surpluses of food. Other populations—such as some groups in central California—actually resisted the introduction of food production because it would have meant a significant reduction in the amount of available food.

Agrarian economies are based on the use of domesticated plants and animals. In some parts of the New World, there were long traditions of using plants and animals that were ultimately domesticated. Food production appears to have archaeological antecedents in these areas, in the sense that we can visualize, at least, a process whereby certain naturally occurring species were brought increasingly under the control of man. In other areas, traditions of using species that were later domesticated appear to be absent. The species either do not occur naturally in these regions, or they appear suddenly and in clearly domesticated forms in the archaeological records. The sudden appearance of these species suggests that the ideas, techniques, and products were introduced from other regions.

In examining the emergence and development of agriculture, we shall first look at the domestication process itself. What changes occur when a species is domesticated? How does this process take place? How does domestication affect the environment in which it occurs? Second, we will consider how nonagricultural societies develop effective agriculture and animal husbandry. What mechanisms are involved in the process? What other changes occur in the social structures as a consequence of this shift? Third, we will see under what conditions a group adopts food-production techniques originally developed elsewhere. How do these innovations spread? What changes occur as a result of their adoption?

PLANTS AND ANIMALS DOMESTICATED IN THE NEW WORLD

In general, the food-producing economies of the New World were based primarily on the exploitation of a series of indigenous, domesticated plants: corn, squashes, potatoes, kidney beans, peanuts, and chili peppers are only a few of the more familiar ones. It is difficult to determine exactly how many plant species were domesticated in the New World, but the number probably exceeds one hundred and fifty. There were only six species of domesticated animals in the New World—dogs, llamas, alpacas, guinea pigs, muscovy ducks, and turkeys—and they were, on the whole, much less important economically than the domesticated animals of the Old World. The Andean region was the only area in the New World where domesticated animals played a major role in the local economies. The achievement of the native Americans was more complex than these numbers indicate. Some species—such as the dog or potato—are composed of many distinct breeds or varieties, each of which might represent an independent domestication.[1]

The native Americans explored and utilized their resources with remarkable thoroughness, for few plants, besides the rubber tree, and no animals indigenous to the New World have been domesticated since the European invasions in the late fifteenth century. They seem to have focused on only a few species from a relatively small number of biological families. For example, more than a dozen of the New World cultivated plants belong to the legume family. From the great majority of New World biological families, no domesticates were produced at all.

The histories of the various New World domesticates are complicated ones, about which we know relatively little. We do know that each domesticate had its own particular geographical distribution and history, which reflect not only the range of environmental conditions that it can adapt to successfully but also the influence of man. Some species—such as the dog, which ranged from the shores of the Arctic Ocean to Tierra del Fuego at the tip of South America—were widespread. Others—the llama or certain Andean food crops, for example—were unknown outside of the areas where they occurred. Finally, a few species, most notably the turkey, were domesticated in one part of their range, Mexico, and wild in the rest of it. Much of the archaeological information concerning early domesticates comes from the arid or semiarid regions of the New World—the American Southwest, the Mexican highlands, and the coast of Peru. Archaeologists have provided us with actual specimens and the biologists have provided us with detailed studies of their genetics, morphology, and so forth. In spite of all of the recent interest in New World domesticates, there are detailed studies of only a few species, usually ones that are economically important at the present time.

Corn is one of the better-known species. All of the different varieties grown today belong to the same species and derive from the same ancestral wild corn. However, the story is complicated. For example, genetic and morphological differences between the

[1]Other domesticates—the llama and alpaca, for example—may not be separate species at all, in the strict biological sense of the term, but rather different breeds of the same one. In this instance, there is some evidence that the llama is, in one sense, a domesticated guanaco and that the alpaca is rather a small llama with exceptionally fine wool. Llamas and alpacas occasionally interbreed with each other at the present time and produce viable offspring, in spite of the fact that they are sometimes classified as different species.

earliest-known domesticated corn in Mexico and that found on the Peruvian coast suggest that the two varieties were domesticated independently; the earliest Mexican corn from the Tehuacán Valley is about 6500 years old by radiocarbon dating, while the earliest domesticated corncobs known in Peru are about 3800 years old. Although direct evidence is lacking, we can probably assume that corn was domesticated independently in other areas as well. Certainly many varieties—such as the ancient Mexican one called Chapalote or some of the recent hybrid dent corns found on the Great Plains—are derived from forms already domesticated.

The archaeological and biological evidence indicates that there was no single center where all plant and animal domestication occurred and that there was no single population responsible for the development of agriculture and animal husbandry. The evidence does indicate that most native American domesticates, particularly the cultivated plants, originated at various places in the vast temperate and tropical region that extends from southern Canada to northern Argentina and that the domestication process occurred more than once in this area, at different times, in different localities, and under the direction of different populations.

The Domestication Process

A question that has interested both archaeologists and biologists is what exactly is involved in the domestication process. How is a wild species transformed into a domesticated one? Judging from the characteristics of today's wild plants and animals, the ancestral species of each New World domesticate must have lived in areas with a certain range of environmental conditions that favored its continued existence. They probably adapted to these conditions in several different ways, and each adaptation that allowed the members of a species to live successfully in a particular environment usually involved a complex of genetic traits rather than just one or two characteristics. Under natural conditions, the members of each species live in populations which tend to interbreed more often with each other than with individuals from another population of the same species. One of the reasons for this is obviously geographical proximity; however, there are also other factors involved.

There is always genetic variability in each breeding population; no two individuals in a particular population are identical. It is possible to describe each breeding population in terms of the frequencies with which certain genetic types occur. For example, in a particular population of wild corn, ten plants out of a thousand, or 1 percent, may have had seeds that were firmly attached to the cob and did not disperse easily, while the remaining 99 percent of the population had seeds that were easily removed from the cob and dispersed by a sudden gust of wind or some other mechanism. In general, populations with many individuals contain more genetic variation and types than those with fewer members. Furthermore, populations that are adapted to a relatively broad range of environmental conditions are usually more variable genetically than those adapted to more limited environmental settings.

From this perspective, each species is composed of a number of distinct, interbreeding populations that may be contiguous or geographically separated. There is obviously some interbreeding, or gene exchange, between different populations of the same species; however, the extent of interbreeding is limited by several factors including geographical isolation or reproductive isolation. Consequently, there are often statistically significant differences in the frequencies with which certain genes occur in different populations. At one extreme are situations where there are marked genetic differences between populations located only a short distance from each other, because each group adapted to the same environment differently or because each adapted to different environmental conditions. At the other extreme are situations where the frequencies of certain genes change gradually in a particular geographical direction, so that the amount of genetic difference between the various populations is directly proportional to the distances separating them. More common, of course, are intermediate situations.

Genetic differences, both within a population and between populations, are the starting point, because hereditary variation is the necessary precondition for all evolutionary change. Evolution occurs when the composition of genetic traits of a population changes with the passage of time. In its most elementary form, evolution consists of changes in gene frequencies. Several factors can alter the proportions of various genes in a population, and, for the purposes of this chapter, the most important of these evolutionary mechanisms is selection.

Selection is basically the nonrandom, differential reproduction of genetically different individuals in a population. This means that, in a particular population, certain genes endow their carriers with slightly better chances of reaching maturity and producing offspring than individuals who lack them. This process operates in two, slightly different ways, depending on the genetic composition of the population and the particular environmental conditions that prevail at the time.

In a population living in a relatively stable environmental setting, where a high proportion of the individuals already carry the beneficial gene complex, the main effect of selection is to eliminate those peripheral individuals who lack the genes of this complex and are consequently less well adapted to that particular environment. In this situation, selection maintains the fitness of the population as a whole by suppressing deviations from the norm. If the environment is changing, however, new selection pressures tend to emerge. Some of the individuals who were peripheral under the old environmental conditions may well possess gene combinations that are now more advantageous than those carried by the old well-adapted group. The old advantageous genes are gradually eliminated from the population, while the new, beneficial ones are preserved and increase proportionately. The rate at which this transformation takes place ultimately depends on the extent of the advantage that the particular genes impart to the individuals who carry them. In this situation, the fitness of the population is maintained as a result of the changes in its genetic composition.

Usually more than one complex of genes is beneficial in a particular environmental setting because of the existence of an array of adaptive goals. This means that several different gene combinations may offer advantages to the individuals who carry them and are exposed to the same selection pressures. If two or more of these gene complexes exist in the same population, then the one that reaches the highest adaptive peak will eventually become the most common one. The possibility of adapting to the same environment in a variety of ways, each involving a different complex of genes, suggests that there are multiple evolutionary pathways; consequently, different populations living in the same environment can evolve in different ways, thus maintaining genetic diversity of the species as a whole.

The process of domestication also involves selection. When human groups were hunting wild animals or harvesting wild plants and using all of this produce as food, the selection pressures on the wild resource populations may not have been significantly different from the ones that would have prevailed under completely natural conditions. However, by the time these groups were keeping small herds of animals and were intentionally planting seeds or cuttings, some of the natural selection pressures were removed from these populations and new ones were unconsciously imposed. The new pressures ultimately led to changes in the genetic compositions of the populations involved. More individuals who were peripheral in the old environmental setting survived to adulthood and reproduced, and the genetic traits advantageous under the new selection pressures became more common in the population. The process of selection operated in the same way in both of the stages described above. What changed from one stage to the other was man's role as an active agent in this environment. This change involved no new knowledge of the environment on his part but rather a redefinition of his place in it.

The key step in plant domestication was the deliberate withholding of seeds or tubers for future planting. This was the new relationship between man and his environment, for it allowed him to increase the availability of certain plant resources in particular localities. What changes were brought about by this new relationship? If man had collected the seeds or tubers randomly from a single population, if he had selected them randomly for planting, and if he had planted a sufficiently large number of them, then the genetic composition of his first domesticated crop would have been very similar to that of its wild parent. This does not seem to have been what happened, however. The seeds or tubers may not have come from a single population but rather from several different ones with various genetic compositions; they may not have been selected randomly for planting; and they probably were not planted where the wild populations occurred but rather in adjacent areas where slightly different environmental conditions and, consequently, selection pressures prevailed. Any one, or all, of these factors would have altered the genetic composition of his first crop.

The Results of Domestication

The first cultivated crops were probably not much more productive, and in some instances, they may even have been less productive than wild stands. Plant cultivation, however, allowed these early food-producing populations to increase significantly the amount of certain plant resources that were available in particular localities. Not only could they harvest the cultivated crop, but they could also collect wild stands of the same species if they existed in the area at all. This increase in both the availability and abundance of plant resources was, of course, limited by droughts and other natural disasters that plague farmers even today in most parts of the world, including such highly developed countries as the United States.

The productivity of these early crops increased once they were cultivated year after year and the processes of unconscious selection began to work on the genetic variation that existed in the different populations that were being tampered with. Larger forms of a species often emerge and compete favorably with smaller wild types when the land in which they are planted is tilled and weeded. Planting itself can lead to selection for forms that germinate rapidly and at roughly the same time or for forms that lack effective mechanisms of seed dispersal and implantation. Harvesting can result in selection for forms with larger fruits or with ineffective seed dispersal mechanisms. It is apparent,

49

both from the early forms that have been found by archaeologists and from their modern descendants, that there was selection for different complexes of genetic traits in different species and in different populations of the same species.

Populations of domesticated plants and animals do not, of course, live in complete isolation in the areas where they occur. There are other species in these regions as well, and the domesticates ultimately compete with them for space and the other resources that are necessary for life. In biological terms, the domesticated and wild species found in the same area are integral parts of an ecosystem. They may be in direct competition for certain resources, or they may exist in some kind of symbiotic relationship with each other. Consequently, the appearance of domesticates or their introduction into an ecosystem must have affected not only the composition of the system but also the relationships that existed among its various parts.

The most obvious consequence of domestication involves changes in the composition of the ecosystem. Certain domesticated species become more abundant in the ecosystem, while the wild species that compete with them directly for the same resources become less common. Eventually, these wild species may disappear altogether in that locality and be replaced entirely by the domesticated one. This process ultimately leads to a reduction in the diversity of the ecosystem as a whole. If agriculture and animal husbandry are practiced with increasing intensity in a particular area, many of the wild species that occurred there originally may be replaced by a much smaller number of domesticated ones. The result is that a relatively generalized ecosystem, composed of a large number of wild species, is transformed into a relatively specialized one, composed of large populations of a few domesticated species and wild forms that live in some sort of symbiotic relationship with them. The productivity of this simplified ecosystem may be significantly greater than it was before, but its diversity and adaptability to new situations have been drastically diminished.

THE EMERGENCE OF AGRICULTURAL ECONOMIES

It is clear that the presence of domesticated plants and animals in an area can significantly increase the amount of food available to its inhabitants. This fact, however, does not satisfactorily answer the question of why some groups found it advantageous or necessary to increase the yields of certain food resources by adopting the practice of domestication, while others did not. In other words, what induced these groups to begin relying on domesticated foods in the first place? A few of the recent answers to this question have emphasized the relationship between population pressure, on the one hand, and the availability and abundance of resources, on the other, as one important factor in the emergence of food-producing economies.

As long as the size of a population remains below the culturally defined carrying capacity of its environment, there is no clear reason for its members to seek new sources of food. However, once the population reaches or surpasses this carrying capacity, the available resources are no longer adequate, as long as patterns of exploitation and consumption remain unchanged. There are several possible solutions to this problem: part of the group can leave the area; the group can alter its patterns of exploitation and utilize the existing resources more intensively or efficiently; or the group can find or create new food resources—the use of domesticated plants and animals is, of course, one way of accomplishing this. According to this explanation for the emergence of food production, population increase leads to a new perception of the environment and its carrying capacity. New aspects of the environment become important, and the carrying capacity is increased because of the additional yields obtained from the domesticated food resources.[2]

This new perception involves a series of shifts in the relative importance of the various food acquisition activities practiced by the population. As agricultural produce becomes increasingly important, the work activities associated with it—clearing fields, planting, weeding, and harvesting—occupy more and more of the group's time. Since these activities must be carried out at particular times of the year, they may ultimately interfere with the acquisition of other food resources that are available during these same periods. Once the group has decided that agriculture is more profitable in the long run, then these other resources and the work activities associated with them begin to diminish in importance. This choice between the relative merits of two or more ways of acquiring food during the same season is called *scheduling.*

Let us now examine the roles played by population pressure, new perceptions of the environment, and the rescheduling of work activities in the transformation of hunting and gathering economies into ones based on effective agricultural production. This process has probably been studied in most detail in the highland valleys of south-central Mexico and on the central coast of Peru. It is already clear from the available archaeological evidence that this transformation occurred in different ways and at different rates in the various areas. In other words, there are multiple pathways leading to the development of effective food-producing economies.

[2]Cf. "Demographic Changes and Environmental Diversity" in Chapter 2.

The Development of an Effective Agrarian Society:
The Tehuacán Valley, Mexico

The ancient inhabitants of the Mexican highlands utilized hundreds of wild species in gaining their livelihood. Some of these resources—such as acorns or pinyon nuts—occurred in one or only a few habitats, while other resources—such as white-tailed deer, maguey, mesquite, or wild corn, to name only a few—were much more widespread and could be found in a large number of different habitats. These widespread resources seem to have been exploited extensively wherever they occurred. Consequently, what distinguishes the economic orientation of one group from that of another is not the widely available resources they used but rather the ones that were available in only limited areas. For instance, groups living in the Oaxaca and Tehuacán Valleys exploited many of the same resources; however, at the height of the winter dry season, the inhabitants of Oaxaca relied on acorns and pinyon nuts collected from the temperate forests of the area, while the *tehuacanos* ate the roots of ceiba trees which were common in some of the xerophytic plant communities of that valley.

The existing population estimates suggest that only six to twelve persons lived in the Tehuacán Valley about 7000 B.C. While this and other population estimates are admittedly speculative, particularly for the early periods, there were relatively few people in the Tehuacán Valley at that time, and they relied on five major resources during the year. In order of decreasing importance, these foods were: first, deer, peccary, antelope, and a few other large game animals; second, a variety of seed-bearing plants and shrubs—amaranth and several species of wild grasses, including corn; third, a number of fruit and pod-bearing trees —avocados, mesquite, and ceiba, to name only three of the more important ones; fourth, rabbits, iguanas, mice, and other small animals that could be trapped easily; and, finally, the so-called starvation plant foods—ceiba roots and maguey and cactus leaves.

The *tehuacanos* did not work to acquire these foods simultaneously or with the same intensity from one season to the next. Instead, their work schedule was geared to the seasonal availability of certain wild plants. For example, during the winter dry season when plant foods were least plentiful and game congregated around the permanent springs, they hunted large animals, trapped smaller ones, and collected maguey leaves and ceiba roots. Between mid-December and mid-March, deer and peccary may have provided as much as three quarters of their total food, while the remainder consisted of small animals, maguey, and ceiba roots. A series of wild plants mature at different times towards the end of the dry season and during the rainy months. From mid-March through mid-September, the *tehuacanos* intensively harvested the produce of these plants, as each ripened in sequence—first, prickly pears and amaranth, then some of the wild grasses and mesquite, and finally, toward the end of the rainy season, many of the wild fruits. Some plants, particularly fruits like prickly pears and avocados, were probably consumed immediately, because they could not be stored effectively for long. Parts of the harvests of plants that could be stored effectively—for example, mesquite, guajes, and the wild grasses —were probably eaten immediately also, while the remaining portions were cached and used later in the year.

The archaeological evidence suggests that plant foods constituted about 65 percent of the diet during these months. Since most of their energy was devoted to plant collecting, the *tehuacanos* had much less time for hunting the large game animals that had retreated back into the hills. Consequently, much of the meat they consumed during these months came from small animals that were trapped or caught in the vicinity of their camps. The period from mid-September to mid-December was a transitional one. Hunting became increasingly important as the animals began to reappear in numbers around the permanent watering places in the valley and as first the fall fruits and then the seeds and pods stored earlier disappeared.

Population Pressure and New Techniques

If the population size had remained constant, this system might have continued indefinitely, because there was enough food available—even during the lean winter months—to feed everyone. This, in fact, did not happen. The number of people living in the Tehuacán Valley grew steadily, increasing to an estimated 200 or 300 by 3000 B.C. In order to deal with a steadily growing population, new ways of providing additional food and increasing the carrying capacity of the environment were devised, either by the local inhabitants themselves or by neighboring groups that faced the same problem. One technique consisted of planting wild fruits—avocados, chupandillas, cosahuicos, and zapotes —around springs and along the banks of streams and rivers. The other technique consisted of sowing a variety of annual seed plants—such as amaranth and corn—in the barrancas or canyons along the edge of the valley. Both practices involved a new perception of the environment; the *tehuacanos* recognized that these plants had requirements that could be satisfied in habitats or localities where they did not occur naturally or in any great abundance. The new perception stressed the agricultural potential of these places rather than whether or not a particular resource occurred in them.

The first fruit trees and annuals that were planted in the valley were probably native to the plant communities of the area. After a short time, however, the *tehuacanos* began importing from neighboring areas many plants which did not grow naturally in their valley. Gourds, squashes, pumpkins, common beans, chili peppers, and tepary beans are only a few of the imports that eventually became important foods in Tehuacán. The imported plants had a number of important consequences. First, they increased the ecological diversity of the valley. Second, because some of them were brought to an environment where they did not occur naturally, new selection pressures were brought to bear on the genetic composition of these populations. Third, the introduction of new varieties of plants that already occurred in the valley undoubtedly increased the genetic variability of the local populations.

Further Consequences of New Techniques

The new techniques of acquiring food—planting fruit trees around permanent sources of water and sowing seeds in and near the barrancas along the edges of the valley—also had a number of consequences. They not only increased the sizes of certain plant populations in the valley but also the probabilities that favorable genetic change would take place in them. It is clear from the plant remains preserved in cave deposits excavated around Tehuacán that yield-increasing genetic changes did occur in these populations. These changes were probably most apparent to the *tehuacanos* in the populations of annual seed plants that mature quickly and have relatively short lifespans—such as corn, amaranth, or chili peppers—and less obvious in the populations of trees that have to grow several years before they bear fruits or pods.

The new techniques also led to larger harvests and, consequently, to an increase in the amount of time and energy that the *tehuacanos* had to devote to agricultural activities. More plant food was available, particularly during the rainy season and immediately after it. Most of the species planted in the barrancas during the spring and early summer matured during the rainy season and could be stored effectively for long periods of time. The fruit trees planted in the well-watered places of the valley ripened, by and large, in the fall months and could not be stored effectively. This produce was probably consumed as soon as it was collected. The increased size of this fall harvest had several important effects. It delayed the time when the population began relying on the seed plants that had been stored during the summer months and, by doing so, postponed the time when the group began to rely on the starvation plants.

As the population of the Tehuacán Valley increased, so did the amount of land under cultivation in or near the barrancas and around the permanent water sources. This implies that the harvests were also considerably larger than they had been earlier. By 3000 B.C., the surpluses remaining from the summer and fall harvests were apparently large enough so that they lasted into the following spring when planting activities began. This development favored the formation of several small villages—composed of about a hundred or so individuals each—that were located along the edges of the valley near barrancas and were occupied continuously throughout the year.

Let us consider briefly how these populations lived at this time. From mid-June to perhaps early October, everyone lived in the villages and devoted virtually all of their time and energy to agricultural pursuits. The only game that was taken during this season consisted of small animals and birds that were probably trapped in the immediate vicinity of the villages or an occasional deer or two that strayed into the valley. From October to mid-June, the population consumed the fall fruits they harvested before beginning to rely on the stored seed plants. Small parties made brief forays into the countryside to hunt, trap, and collect wild seeds, fruits, and leaves that were available during the dry season in order to supplement the plant foods that were cached in the villages.

During the next two millennia, the population increased steadily, so that an estimated 1000 to 1500 persons lived in the valley by about 800 B.C. The number of villages located along the edges of the valley increased from two to five. The amount of land under cultivation also increased; however, there were limits to the amount of land that could be farmed with the agricultural systems used by the *tehuacanos*. Farming was feasible only in and near the barrancas and around well-watered places; the greater part of the valley was not farmed under these agricultural systems. Furthermore, the fields that were cultivated produced only one crop each year. Once all of the available localities were under cultivation, the possibilities of significantly increasing yields were considerably diminished. The only ways to increase harvests were to plant new combinations of cultigens that might produce slightly higher yields or to wait and hope for yield-increasing genetic changes in the cultivated species. Given the *tehuacanos'* perception of their environment, the carrying capacity of the valley was either being rapidly approached or even somewhat strained by this time.

Irrigation Agriculture

To meet the continually increasing demands for food, a more intensive land use system based on irrigation agriculture was

55

introduced into the Tehuacán Valley about 800 B.C. Irrigation canals carried water from the river and permanent springs and, later, from man-made reservoirs to fields located in many parts of the valley that had not been farmed earlier. This innovation involved a radically different perception of the environment, which ultimately led to a tremendous increase in the carrying capacity of the valley. No longer was it necessary to farm only in those places where water and certain other resources occurred. Instead, these resources could be brought to parts of the valley where they did not occur naturally. As a result, virtually the entire valley became potential farmland rather than just those areas around the barrancas and permanent water sources.

Harvests increased significantly, merely because there was much more farmland in the valley. The *tehuacanos* continued to farm around the barrancas and permanent water sources at the same time as they began to cultivate more of the newly opened lands. These larger yields may have increased the nutritional level of the society as a whole, which would have led to further population growth. It appears that the population of the Tehuacán Valley grew steadily from 1000 to 1500 persons to an estimated 4000 to 5000 at the beginning of the Christian Era and eventually to about 100,000 at the time of the Spanish conquest.

The food supply was relatively elastic during this period. At first, the *tehuacanos* may have grown only a single crop each year on their new farmlands. However, as the population and demand for additional food increased, they began to use the land more intensively, growing two or three crops a year on the same plot. The intensive land use system that was emerging in the valley had a number of implications concerning the amount of labor that was invested in agricultural pursuits and the seasonal availability of cultivated plant foods.

When two or three crops were produced each year on the same plot of land, the *tehuacanos* had to devote more time and energy to agrcultural labor than before. The fields had to be prepared two or three times a year rather than once; they had to be planted each time; they had to be weeded and watered more often; and each crop had to be harvested. They had to perform other activities associated with agriculture as well—for example, the irrigation canals had to be cleaned frequently and the damaged sections repaired. Among other things, this meant that those individuals engaged in agricultural pursuits had less time to devote to other activities than they had before. The fact that agricultural laborers were working harder and more regularly, combined with the steadily increasing population, may have facilitated greater divisions of labor within the society.

The *tehuacanos* no longer relied exclusively on stored surpluses to carry them through the winter dry season, for cultivated plant foods were now grown and available throughout the year. During the winter months, they harvested seed crops—corn, beans, squash, and chili peppers—from the irrigated fields of the valley. Another crop of seed plants was harvested from the irrigated fields toward the end of the dry season at about the same time as amaranth was ripening in the areas around the barrancas. During the summer months, crops were planted in both the barranca areas and the irrigated fields; these were harvested as they became available. In the fall months, the inhabitants of the valley also harvested both the wild and cultivated fruits that grew in the valley. Throughout the year, these foods were supplemented occasionally with game, small animals, and a few wild plants that may have been gathered by individuals who devoted part or all of their time to these activities rather than engaging in agricultural pursuits.

The ecology of the Tehuacán Valley was gradually transformed as the patterns of land use became more intensive and the amount of agricultural land increased. The natural plant formations that formerly existed in the cultivated areas were replaced by a relatively small number of highly productive domesticated species. Some of the wild species that were common in the valley before the advent of effective food production probably disappeared altogether, while others survived only in small relic communities located in the isolated or infrequently used portions of the valley.

Earlier in this section, it was suggested that effective agricultural production emerged in various ways in different parts of the New World. The particular process that occurred in the Tehuacán Valley, where agriculture could have been practiced only during the rainy season before the introduction of water control or water management systems, was probably very different from the developments that took place in areas such as the Gulf Coast of Mexico or the Amazon Basin, where farming could have been practiced throughout the year. It was also very different from the process that occurred in areas where virtually all of the cultigens, and probably the agricultural technology as well, were borrowed from neighboring areas.

The Spread of Agricultural Innovations: The Ancón-Chillón Region

The emergence of effective food-producing economies in some parts of the New World depended more on the adoption of agricultural innovations that originated elsewhere than it did on the further development or refinement of existing food acquisition activities. This pattern of economic change probably occurred most often in areas where the various regional populations had significantly different economic orientations because of the kinds of resources that were available and used. A few regional populations in these areas may have obtained some of their food by farming—perhaps in much the same manner as the early inhabitants of the Tehuacán Valley—while the remainder based their livelihoods on other kinds of food acquisition activities.

The Borrowing Process

The agricultural innovations adopted consisted of new domesticated foodstuffs, tools, techniques, and ideas that, once adopted by groups that did not practice farming, ultimately led to a new perception of the environment and its resources and to an increase in the amount of food available by increasing production per capita. Production per capita is not, of course, a simple product of the amount of time and energy that an individual spends producing this food. A farmer may have access to twice as much food as a hunter or gatherer, but he may have to work three or four times as many hours to get it.

Agricultural innovations spread from the peoples who developed them or adopted them early in the diffusion process to various groups of potential users. Each innovation had its own place of origin and pattern of spread as it moved from regions where it was in common use to others where it was unknown or rarely used. The new items spread at different rates and were adopted at different times as the various groups became aware of them and interested in their possibilities. Many factors besides strictly economic considerations were involved in the acceptance of new innovations, judging by the long delays that occurred before some items with demonstrable economic advantages were finally adopted. For example, some sorghum farmers in the midwestern United States were slow to adopt new, high-yield varieties, because to do so would have meant that they had to modify their traditional agricultural practices.

The flow of agricultural innovations into an area can increase the perceived carrying capacity of that environment, providing a basis for even further demographic expansion, and can promote a wide variety of social changes—for instance, performing new kinds of work activities or settling in new localities. This is what happened in many parts of coastal Peru between three and five thousand years ago, when the resident populations of the area adopted a series of agricultural innovations that originated in the mountain valleys and lowland areas to the east. As an example of the kind of transformation that can take place under these conditions, let us briefly consider what happened in the Ancón-Chillón region on the central coast of Peru.

The estimated population of this region was about fifty to one hundred persons around 3000 B.C. From June to October, this group lived in the Ancón *lomas*—an area covered with wild grasses and succulent plants that were watered by the heavy fogs which blanket the desert coast during the winter months. Judging by the food remains that have been found in sites dating to this period, the population relied extensively on the seasonal plant resources of the *lomas*—wild grasses, potatoes, and other tubers —and to a lesser extent on the game and birds that also wintered in this habitat. The group also relied for a considerable part of its food on the year-round resources of the ocean—fish, shellfish, and several species of edible marine plants.

Summer season habitation sites dating to this period have not yet been identified in the Ancón-Chillón area; however, they have been found in several nearby areas, and we can use this information to reconstruct the general outlines of what the Ancón population did during the rest of the year. These data suggest that the members had two alternatives. First, a small portion of the group may have summered in the high grasslands of the mountains where game animals were abundant. Second, a larger portion of the population moved into the lower part of the Chillón Valley, where they gathered wild plants from the valley floor and riverbanks, caught crayfish in the river, hunted and trapped small animals, collected marine shellfish, fished off the rocky points along the shore, and perhaps even harvested a few cultivated gourds and squash that grew along the edge of the river.

Although the population relied considerably on the seasonal resources of a variety of terrestrial and riverine habitats, it is clear that its members were exploiting the year-round resources of the ocean much more efficiently and intensively than their predecessors in the area. In fact, the bulk of the meat protein they consumed during the year was probably derived from marine products; this possibly raised the nutritional level of the society as a whole and ultimately led to an increase in its size. By 2500 B.C., the population of the Ancón-Chillón area seems to have doubled, and a new economic orientation was beginning to emerge.

Population Pressure and New Orientations

This new orientation was based largely on the intensive and efficient exploitation of a limited number of resources—those found in the marine and littoral habitats. During the next six hundred years, the exploitation of these habitats became so efficient and intensive that the resources of some shellfish beds were completely depleted, while the productivity of several other beds was substantially diminished. Year-round settlements, with populations of fifty to one hundred individuals each, at first were located in close proximity to these resource areas. As time passed, the number of these oceanside villages increased from two to three, and the population of each may eventually have reached several hundred individuals. The locations of these settlements actually facilitated the exploitation of marine resources—particularly shellfish—which are concentrated in relatively small areas, because they brought together large numbers of people in the immediate vicinity of the habitats and reduced the amount of economically unprofitable time that they spent traveling between their homes and the places where food was found.

Plant cultivation became increasingly important between 2500 and 1900 B.C. on the central Peruvian coast. This activity was carried on by small populations—perhaps no more than two or three families from each of the coastal fishing villages—that lived in the lower part of the Chillón Valley near places where the river overflowed its banks between late December and early February. These groups planted chili peppers, common beans, guavas, gourds, several kinds of squash, and cotton along the banks of the river or in the rich soils of the floodplains. All of these crops, with the possible exception of cotton, were first domesticated elsewhere in South America and then adopted on the central coast. Since planting and harvesting times were almost entirely dependent on the level of the river during this period, the inland populations produced only a single crop each year. These groups fished when they were not engaged in agricultural activities, judging by the broken and unfinished shell fishhooks that have been found in one of the inland sites. They also sent large portions of their harvest to the inhabitants of the coastal fishing villages which were located where plant cultivation was impossible.

Later Stages

By 1900 B.C., the population of the Ancón-Chillón area had risen to an estimated 1000 to 1500 persons. Perhaps four hundred of these lived in a pair of coastal fishing villages composed of several hundred individuals each. The economic orientation of these fishing communities was not significantly different from that of their ancestors. They fished off the rocky points and along the beaches of the coast and collected shellfish from beds in both habitats. These activities provided the bulk of the protein consumed by the coastal populations; this was supplemented by a few shore birds—pelicans, gulls, and cormorants—and mammals. In the habitation refuse deposits at these villages, there was also a considerable increase in both the quantity and variety of cultivated plants that were brought from the inland parts of the valley.

Virtually all of the rest of the population—perhaps 500 to 1000 persons—lived in a large inland settlement located about a mile from the ocean near most of the arable land along the river in the lower part of the Chillón Valley. Judging by the remains of food found in the garbage dumps at this site, plant cultivation may have been as important in the daily lives of its inhabitants as either fishing or shellfish collecting between November and late May. Nearly all of the cultivated plants that were used by the inhabitants of this site, as well as those of the coastal villages, could have been grown along the banks of the river in the lower part of the Chillón Valley.

The remainder of the population lived in very small settlements in the middle part of the Chillón Valley at varying distances from the sea. These groups—consisting of two or three families each—were engaged mainly in agricultural pursuits. They probably grew a variety of food plants that were adapted to diverse conditions but specialized in one or two crops—such as coca or avocados—that were most productive in the environment in the middle of this valley. Agriculture based on seasonal rainfall was impossible or impractical depending on the elevation of the particular settlement, because precipitation is either highly irregular or absent altogether in these localities. Riverbank agriculture would also have been difficult, if not impossible, because the rivers have cut deep channels, and floodplains are either exceedingly small or nonexistent in this area. Consequently, any agricultural activity near these settlements probably involved the use of short canals that brought water from the river to the lands situated above it. Since water is always available in the Chillón River, these lands could have been watered throughout the year, and more than one crop could have been harvested. At first, these groups may have harvested only one crop each year, but, as the demand for more food increased, they could have intensified their use of the land, taking two and perhaps three crops a year from it.

Thus, the economy of the Ancón-Chillón population during this period was composed of three distinct parts: fishing and shellfish gathering on the coast, single-crop riverbank and floodplain agriculture in the lower part of the valley, and possibly multi-crop irrigation agriculture with emphasis on particular plant foods in the middle part of the valley. These sectors were bound together by a redistribution or exchange system which made marine products available to the inland populations, particularly those living at considerable distances from the coast, and plant foods available to the inhabitants of the coastal villages. What distinguishes this exchange network from the earlier one that existed in the area are the number of geographically distinct groups that participated in the redistribution system and the greater quantity and variety of goods from distant resource areas that appear in the habitation refuse deposits at the various settlements.

After 1750 B.C., the land use system employed by the inhabitants of the lower part of the Chillón Valley became more intensive, as they gradually adopted a small water management system for irrigation agriculture and continued to farm along the banks of the river. At first, the irrigation canals were probably quite short—perhaps no more than three or four miles in length; however, the use of even a single short canal would have tripled or quadrupled the amount of arable land. The water management system introduced into the lower valley, possibly by the inhabitants of the middle valley, was gradually enlarged through time. It probably reached its maximum extent and essentially its present form about A.D. 450, when the population of the lower valley may have been around 30,000 to 40,000 persons, judging by the total area covered by archaeological sites dating from this time in comparison with the size of the modern settlements.

What emerged on the central Peruvian coast towards the end of the third millennium B.C. was a highly diversified economy with a continually growing number of part-time or full-time farmers and fishermen. At first, the economy was based on the exploitation of marine products that were available throughout the year. These resources provided a permanent food base for the inhabitants of the area that allowed some of them to divert their attention to other activities. These resources were supplemented by an ever increasing quantity and variety of domesticated foodstuffs that were grown in the valley lands. As time passed and agricultural produce became an increasingly important source of food, a greater proportion of the total population became involved in agricultural activities. At the same time, the proportion of the population, though perhaps not the total number of individuals, involved in marine and littoral harvesting diminished.

Once the residents of the central coast of Peru began to accept agricultural innovations, it took them only a relatively brief period of time to develop an effective food-producing economy—much shorter, in fact, than the inhabitants of the Tehuacán Valley and perhaps other areas where indigenous species were originally brought under domestication. There are several obvious reasons for this. First, the population was already exploiting permanently available marine resources that could support a relatively large number of people. Second, the agricultural innovations, which increased the amount of food available, were easily assimilated into the existing economic activities of the population. Third, sustained population growth in the area allowed a continually increasing number of people to divert their attention to agricultural production which further increased the amount of food available.

The basic agricultural implement in both areas was probably the digging stick. For their planting techniques, we have to rely on ethnographic analogies with later groups: they may have burned off the vegetation where they planted or they may have dug it out with digging sticks. We have very little evidence about how food was stored in either Tehuacán or the Ancón-Chillón region during these earlier periods, because virtually all of the excavations in both areas were made in garbage dumps. In the Oaxaca Valley of Mexico, where part of a village dating between 1200 and 800 B.C. was excavated, the inhabitants stored food in pits outside of their houses; however, we lack evidence from the Tehuacán and Ancón-Chillón regions that their inhabitants did the same thing with food. Food preparation techniques are also uncertain at this time. Roasting was probably important during the earlier periods in both areas; in fact, we have evidence of clambakes from coastal Peru. The food remains collected in both areas consist of bone fragments, unprocessed plants (beans, corncobs with the kernels in place and removed, etc.), and human feces. Food remains have been identified in feces from both areas, but these have been so altered by mastication and digestive juices that we have no idea how the food was prepared, only that it was consumed.

CONCLUSION: MODELS OF AGRICULTURAL DEVELOPMENT AND INTERREGIONAL EXCHANGE

The Tehuacán Valley and the Ancón-Chillón region provide models of how effective food-producing economies developed in two different kinds of areas: a highland one where some of the indigenous wild species were ultimately domesticated and a coastal one where the ideas of agriculture and animal husbandry were essentially borrowed from the outside. It is clear that there were several significant differences between the two models.

First, the initial stages of each were characterized by slightly different patterns of resource exploitation. The coastal economic orientation relied fairly intensively on marine protein foods available at any time of the year, while the highland one focused largely on seasonally available plant foods. One implication of this difference was that the coastal environment could support a larger population than the highland area, because its carrying capacity was greater. Second, agriculture appeared much earlier in the highlands and took much longer to develop into effective food production than it did on the coast. There are probably many reasons for this; the coastal groups imported already developed plants and techniques and, consequently, did not have to spend much time experimenting with them, and they had a much larger potential labor force, at least part of which could be diverted almost immediately into part-time or full-time farming without diminishing the nutritional level of the group as a whole. Third, the population growth rate was considerably higher on the coast than in the highlands, before agricultural production appeared and during its early stages of development. This probably relates to the kinds of resources that were being used when agriculture first appeared in the two areas and to the role it played in the economies as a whole. Fourth, economic specialization appeared much earlier on the coast and developed more rapidly, because new kinds of work activities were added to the ones that were already being practiced.

These two models do not describe how agricultural production appeared in every part of the New World. Archaeological investigations that are now being carried out in the American Southwest, the Illinois River Valley, Oaxaca, and the central highlands of Peru strongly suggest that agricultural economies developed differently in these areas than in either the Tehuacán Valley or the Ancón-Chillón region. When they are completed, we should have half a dozen or so different models describing the emergence of food-producing economies instead of the two mentioned above. They will provide us with a much better understanding of the range of variation involved in the appearance of agriculture and allow us to deal more adequately with the problems of whether the same processes were operating in each area and whether these interacted with each other in the same manner.

The evidence from the central Peruvian highlands is also interesting when it is examined in terms of what is already known about the archaeology of the central coastal region of that country. At the present time, Peru is the only place in the world where detailed investigations of the development of agricultural economies have been carried out in adjacent areas with very different environmental settings. The evidence indicates that there was virtually continuous exchange between the coastal and highland areas from the time man first entered the Andes to the present and that the nature and volume of this exchange varied considerably from one period to the next. It also indicates that exchange between regions with very different natural endowments, population densities, social structures, and economic orientations played a very prominent role in producing the kinds of institutions, ideas, and settlement patterns that characterized the central Andes. Raw materials, agricultural produce, and technology were not the only items moving through this exchange network. Equally, if not more, important were ideas—such as those concerning how communities should be organized or what settlements should be like.

4. Settlements

People space themselves in various ways over the landscape in order to carry out certain activities efficiently. These include food acquisition, industry, commerce, and services, if we define the last term broadly enough to include such diverse things as religious, cultural, artistic, or political activities. They are the reasons for a settlement's existence, and each of them is independent in that it does not necessarily have to be performed in the same place as the others.

THE DIVERSITY OF SETTLEMENTS

Consequently, there were many different kinds of settlements in the New World, and no single one adequately serves as a descriptive model for all of the others. There were settlements occupied continuously throughout the year and ones occupied only during particular seasons or on special occasions. In some settlements only a single activity was performed and in others many different activities took place. Many settlements had as few as a dozen inhabitants and several had more than 100,000. There were dispersed settlements with widely separated buildings and nucleated settlements where all of the buildings were close together. There were settlements where all of the inhabitants belonged to the same ethnic group and ones where they belonged to different ethnic groups. Even contemporary settlements in the same region were often quite different from each other. Let us now look at some of the factors that produced this diversity of settlement forms.

The Location of Settlements

From a rather narrow economic perspective, the minimal requirements for life are really quite few. A group must have access to food, water, fuel, and raw materials for building and making tools. In any region, the distribution of these resources is fixed by the prevailing natural conditions and by the inhabitants' perception of their environment. Different groups may perceive the environment differently or attach different relative values to its resources. For instance, one group may consider immediate access to water more important than the immediate availability of other basic resources, and as a result, its members settle near a spring or lake. Their contemporaries in the same region may consider that the immediate availability of water is less important than immediate access to food, so they establish themselves near food resource areas, which may be located at a considerable distance from the nearest source of water.

Groups space themselves throughout an area to exploit the basic resources in the proportions they need to sustain themselves. Because of the different perceptions of resources or the different relative values assigned to them, different groups may space themselves differently in the same area. Therefore, the location of settlements is variable and reflects not only the patterns of resource exploitation but also the relative importance attached to each of the resources that is being used. If the members of a group behave rationally in an economic sense, then they will establish their settlements where they can minimize costs and maximize profits. Suppose a group with a given economic orientation moves into an area and finds that there are two possible places where its members can establish their settlement. Before they establish this settlement, however, they must weigh the economic advantages and disadvantages of each locality in terms of the resources they exploit, how often they use each resource, and how far they must travel to acquire each of them. Such a decision may affect not only the location of the settlement but also the rest of its form.

Let us consider how these factors affected the location of actual settlements on the central coast of Peru about 5000 B.C. The oldest known year-round settlement in the area dates from this time and is located in the lower Lurín Valley. Its inhabitants collected wild foods from the resource areas around their settlement. Some of the foods they used—like fish and marine molluscs—were available throughout the year, while others—sea lions, river crayfish, or *lomas* grasses and tubers—were available only during particular seasons. What made this group unique at this time was not so much its choice of foods as its choice of a place to settle in order to acquire them. The area around the village was ecologically diverse, so that all of the resources needed were nearby. The settlement was in a place where virtually all of the resource areas used by the inhabitants were contiguous with each other; as a result, they never had to travel

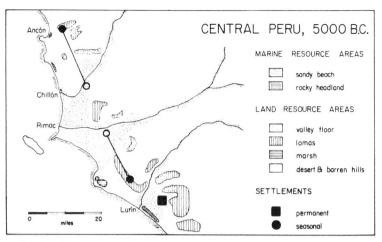

Fig. 4–1. The locations of settlements and resource areas on the central coast of Peru at 5000 B.C. The open settlement symbols represent hypothetical summer camps located in areas of intensive cultivation or dense contemporary settlement. They are postulated on the basis of firm archaeological evidence from a nearby coastal valley.

more than three and a half miles, roughly an hour's walk, in any direction to obtain what they needed.

Their contemporaries fifty miles to the north in the Ancón-Chillón area were not able to maintain year-round settlements in their territory. They exploited essentially the same wild foods as their neighbors to the south, although they may have placed somewhat greater importance on certain seasonal resources. What prevented them from establishing a permanent settlement in this region was the spacing of seasonal food resource areas. The summer resources were concentrated at one end of their territory and the winter resources at the other. The two areas were separated by a twelve-mile-wide stretch of coastal desert where no food was available at any time of the year. The cost in time of traveling with any regularity between these places was too great, so the group chose to live in two seasonal settlements. One was located where seasonal resources were particularly plentiful during the winter, and the other was in an area where seasonal resources were abundant during the summer. By moving back and forth between the two localities, the group was max-imizing its profits and minimizing its costs, just as the population to the south did by remaining in one settlement all year.

There are other factors, besides strictly economic ones, that can influence the location of settlements. Defensive considera-tions, the avoidance of disease-ridden places, the availability of the broadly defined services mentioned earlier, and tradition are only a few of the more obvious social factors influencing settle-

67

ment location. Such factors have two important effects. First, they reduce the number of possible localities for settlements. And second, they require that the members of a group weigh the social advantages and disadvantages of each locality, as well as the economic ones, in their analysis of profits and costs.

In recent years, it has become increasingly clear that the time and distance required for travel to the resources and facilities group members use are more important in determining the location and form of their settlements than are either their technical achievements or the environment in which they live. The relationship between distance and travel time probably varies with topography, ground cover, mode of transportation, and so forth. In Peru, for example, it is possible to walk about three and a half miles in an hour. Any distance up to about two thirds of a mile, roughly fifteen minutes, appears to be relatively unimportant in that it requires little or no adjustment of the patterns of settlement and the use of resources and facilities. Some kind of minor adjustment of these patterns may be necessary when slightly greater travel times and distances are involved. Beyond about three and a half miles, an hour's walk in the Peruvian environments, the cost of movement becomes high enough that there must be some sort of major adjustment of these patterns. This accommodation can take a variety of forms—for example, the establishment of subsidiary settlements, the maintenance of residences in more than one locality, participation in some sort of regional exchange network, or movement from one place to another during particular seasons or on special occasions.

Changes in Settlement Location and Form: The Rimac Valley

Settlement locations and forms change continuously, usually as somewhat delayed responses to the appearance of new social, economic, and political conditions in the surrounding area. The rate at which these changes occur varies considerably, depending on how fast the new conditions emerge and how influential they are. A good example of this comes from the middle part of the Rimac Valley in central Peru, where there was a series of four very distinctive settlement locations and forms between A.D. 1400 and 1600 that reflected the changing political and economic conditions of the area.

From A.D. 1400 to about 1500, the inhabitants of the region lived in a small dispersed settlement composed of fairly large houses built on stone-faced platforms on the lower slopes of the hills overlooking the valley floor. They farmed the arable land on the valley floor and probably exchanged some of their produce with kinsmen who lived up the valley in slightly different ecological settings where different varieties of crops could be grown. In times of trouble, perhaps when attacks from outsiders who lived down the valley were imminent, they retreated to a hilltop fort more than 2000 feet above the valley floor.

The population was incorporated, apparently peacefully, into the Inca Empire about A.D. 1470, and was considered a valued ally by the Incas. However, the Incas maintained close control over their subjects, allies or not, and they moved the inhabitants of this area into a nucleated settlement where they could better watch and control their activities. The new houses were contiguous and about two thirds the size of the earlier ones. New building complexes were also erected at two nearby localities. One, about 500 yards from the village, was probably the seat of Inca political control in the area. It consisted of a set of stone-faced drying terraces, lines of storehouses, and a house compound with a large proportion of broken imitation Inca pottery scattered around it. The other building complex, about 500 yards from the storehouses and 1000 yards from the village, consisted of four platform mounds surrounding a rectangular plaza. This complex was probably a shrine dedicated to a locally important oracle mentioned in sixteenth-century historical documents. During this period, the settlement consisted of three functionally distinct parts separated from each other by large tracts of arable land.

The power of the Inca government waned quickly after the arrival of the Spaniards and, by 1535, it was replaced by that of a Spanish conqueror, who supposedly protected the native population and provided them with religious instruction in return for their tribute and labor. He apparently lived in the capital city about thirty miles away and had little concern with where and how the local population lived as long as its members provided the tribute and labor he required. His control over the population was probably exercised largely through the traditional native leaders of the area. One consequence of this new situation was that the remnants of the local population abandoned the nucleated village where they lived during the period of Inca rule and returned to their traditional homes on the hillslopes bordering the valley floor.

During the 1570's, the native populations of this and other parts of the middle Rimac Valley were forced to move into a new settlement by the Spaniards. It was patterned after a Spanish town with a church, jail, and government house located on three sides of a plaza at one end of the settlement and a grid system of streets. By concentrating the native population in a single place, making them live in houses with single entrances that opened onto the streets, and requiring them to return there at the end of each day's work, the Spanish civil and religious authorities who

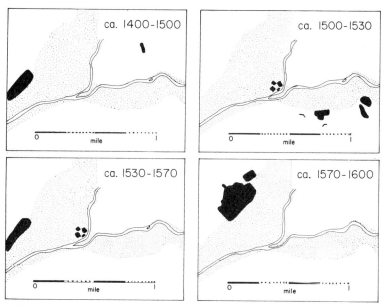

Fig. 4–2. Changes in the location and form of settlements in the middle Rimac Valley of central Peru.

now resided in the town were able to watch their activities more closely—to ensure that the full amount of the required tribute was paid and to prevent or reduce the possibility of a native rebellion.

The social and economic conditions of the middle Rimac Valley changed significantly between A.D. 1400 and 1600, as effective political control passed first from the traditional native leaders to the Incas, back to the traditional leaders who served as intermediaries for the Spaniards, and finally to the Spaniards. These changes are reflected in the sequence of settlement forms and their locations in the area. Each group—the native population, the Incas, and the Spaniards—had its own conception of what a settlement should be like, and they applied or imposed their own views whenever they had effective political control over the area. By examining the various forms and locations of settlement that existed in a particular area and the sequence in which they occurred, we can learn a great deal about the people who lived there and how their ideas and perceptions were transformed by the appearance of new conditions.

The Functions of Settlements

The inhabitants of a given settlement may perform a great variety of different activities or only a few. These may be practiced by full-time specialists or only occasionally by individuals who are primarily engaged in other pursuits. Some of these activities may benefit only the residents of the settlement itself, while others may benefit the members of some larger community of people.

The farming and fishing settlements of the Ancón-Chillón area, mentioned in the last chapter, provide an excellent example of this. The coastal fishing villages were located near rich shellfish beds and fishing grounds, which their inhabitants exploited efficiently. Since agriculture was not possible around the fishing villages, all of the cultivated plant foods consumed by their inhabitants were grown in the inland parts of the Chillón Valley by groups that were beginning to specialize in agricultural production. In exchange for the plant foods they received, the coastal fishermen sent marine produce to the inland populations. This exchange network was relatively small in the sense that it probably never took more than three or four days for produce to move between the most distant populations participating in the system. However, the fact that even a small-scale exchange system had developed in this area by 1900 B.C. facilitated the continued existence of these economically specialized settlements on a year-round basis.

Often, a particular settlement was established to fulfill certain needs or wants that existed under a given set of social and economic conditions. As either these wants or conditions changed, it may have become increasingly difficult or even impossible for its residents to continue performing the activities they were carrying out, and, eventually, the settlement declined or disappeared altogether. The ghost mining towns of the western United States and Canada that were virtually abandoned after their mineral deposits were exhausted or the Inca administrative centers in Peru, like Huánuco Viejo, that were rapidly depopulated after the collapse of Inca political control are only two of the many examples of this process.

Nevertheless, some settlements do continue to exist in spite of changing social and economic conditions. Their inhabitants may substitute new activities for old ones or add new activities to those that already exist. They may continue to maintain commercial or exchange relationships with the population of the surrounding area, or they may even expand these relationships to include a greater number of people.

This is apparently what happened at Pachacamac on the central coast of Peru after about A.D. 1450. For several centuries prior to this time, there was an oracle at Pachacamac that probably had no more than local importance. However, about the time that the Incas began to incorporate larger and larger numbers of people into their empire, the influence of Pachacamac—both the oracle

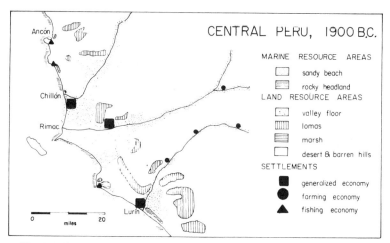

Fig. 4–3. The locations of settlements and resource areas on the central coast of Peru at 1900 B.C.

and the settlement—began to increase as well. After the Incas incorporated the area around Pachacamac into their empire, the influence of the oracle increased considerably. Branch oracles were established in half a dozen or more localities throughout the Inca Empire, and the oracle at Pachacamac began collecting tribute from as far away as the northern coast of Ecuador which was, at best, peripheral to the area where the Incas had effective political control. The priests associated with the oracle at Pachacamac were exporting a socially beneficial product—predictions concerning the outcomes of various courses of action in the future. In return for these prophecies, they received economically valuable goods—such as fine cloth, herds of llamas, and precious metals. Their ability to increase their sphere of influence was probably both created and enhanced by the growth of the Inca Empire.

Archaeologists have long been interested in what happens in year-round settlements, particularly in those large nucleated ones that we call towns or cities. Such settlements have a number of characteristics. First, they have relatively large stable populations that remain in one place for long periods of time rather than a continual turnover of residents. Second, the members of these populations perform a wide variety of activities rather than just one or two. Third, people are in the settlements for many different reasons, including commerce, residence, or to use the goods, services, and facilities available. Fourth, both the residents and the transients share the facilities and services that are available. In other words, these settlements are distinguished by their size, permanency, and diversity.

The reason for the archaeologists' interest in large, nucleated settlements with relatively dense, stable populations is not that life in them was somehow better or more advanced than life in other kinds of settlements. In fact, there is considerable evidence accumulated from various parts of the world that life in permanent nucleated settlements, particularly in the larger ones, may actually have been less healthy than life in small settlements or dispersed ones because of the opportunities for disease and epidemics resulting from pollution, poor sanitary conditions, and crowding. In spite of these and probably other limitations, large nucleated settlements with permanent populations can, under certain conditions, offer at least one important opportunity to their inhabitants. They can be centers where innovations—new ideas, techniques, and tools—are more likely to occur and ultimately be incorporated into the daily lives and activities of their inhabitants. These innovations can, in turn, act as a trigger for further social and economic changes in the surrounding areas.

The innovative process consists essentially of using or combining ideas, techniques, or tools in novel ways. The flow of information increases in situations where people with different cultural or social backgrounds have access to each other, communicate and collaborate with each other, and live in a social environment where there is an expectation of change within certain prescribed segments of behavior. The existence of these conditions is far more important in the innovative process than the size or density of population. When they exist, innovations are likely to occur more often in large nucleated settlements than in small or dispersed ones simply because they contain a greater number of people who have to deal with each other, at least minimally, on some sort of face-to-face basis. As a result, any one individual potentially has contact with a greater number of people and more frequent occasion to exchange ideas and information with them than his counterpart living in the countryside. Just by chance alone, there is a greater likelihood that innovations will appear in large nucleated settlements where the appropriate social and cultural conditions prevail.

The Internal Structure of Settlements: Tenochtitlán and Cuzco

The opportunities for innovations to occur can be either limited or enhanced by the internal structures of nucleated settlements. In order to elaborate on this point, let us contrast the effects that the internal structures of two settlements had on the innovative process. One of the settlements is Tenochtitlán, the capital of the Aztec Empire in Mexico, and the other is Cuzco, the capital of the Inca Empire in the central Andes. Both settlements are known from archaeological and historical sources, and both have often been referred to as cities.

Tenochtitlán had a population of 150,000 to 200,000 persons on the eve of the Spanish invasion. Many of the residents were immigrants from other areas—craft specialists, individuals from subject groups who had special privileges or were required to spend part of each year in the Aztec capital, and refugees who had been displaced by war. These outsiders were readily accepted and integrated into the local population and apparently lived in various parts of the city. In addition, tens of thousands of people came to the city on market days or arrived with tribute from various subjugated regions. They often remained in the city for days or even weeks and were accommodated in different ways; some had their own houses, while others stayed in Aztec households or in buildings that functioned as hotels.

The inhabitants of Tenochtitlán worked at many different occupations. Historical accounts mention military, administrative, religious, commercial, and craft specialists who resided in different areas. The city itself was divided into quarters, each with its own market, shrine, and other facilities. These, in turn, were divided into districts, or *barrios,* which also had their own markets, shrines, and facilities. Consequently, there was a great deal of duplication and diversity within the city. For example, a goldsmith from one of the subjugated provinces might reside next to an Aztec bureaucrat, and both would use many of the same public facilities that were available in their *barrio,* while individuals living in another district would use the facilities located there. On certain occasions, all of them might use the public facilities of their quarter of the city or even those of the city itself. In addition, the goldsmith and the bureaucrat might belong to guilds that had their shrines in other parts of the city.

One of the first Spaniards to see the Inca capital of Cuzco estimated that it contained 4000 residential buildings; although his estimate may be high, it is clear that there were a lot of buildings in the settlement and that its population was substantial. The city was laid out in the shape of a puma, with a fortress representing its head and a large public square occupying the space between its front and back legs. The area around the city contained a substantial number of residential settlements and storehouses, some of which were considered to be part of the city itself. It is clear that the last four Inca emperors maintained palaces in the city, as well as country estates in the area around it. Furthermore, the most important nobles from the conquered provinces maintained houses in Cuzco and were required to live there for four months each year along with their servants. There were also at least three major shrines in the city that were served by professional priests, who presumably lived in the capital, and a convent.

An early historical account emphasized that no poor people lived in the city, which suggests that no individuals, except servants, who did not belong to the nobility resided there. The non-nobles, craftsmen and specialists working for the state, and visitors apparently lived in the various residential settlements around the capital and utilized the state-controlled public facilities that were available in the city and its environs.

There are some striking contrasts between the internal structures of the two settlements. First, Cuzco was organized in such a way that there was a major distinction between the city proper and the residential settlements surrounding it, while Tenochtitlán was divided internally into a number of more or less identical districts. Second, there was much greater social diversity in Tenochtitlán than Cuzco; the inhabitants of a typical district in the Aztec capital came from a wider variety of backgrounds and had a broader range of experiences presumably than the Inca and provincial elite who resided in Cuzco proper. Third, there was much more duplication of public facilities in Tenochittlán than Cuzco; this provided an opportunity, at least, for variations to develop in the ways in which things were carried out in different parts of the city. Fourth, Cuzco was organized in such a way that each part of the city served a particular function, while Tenochtitlán was organized so that each district served a variety of functions which ensured that people would be in the same locality at different times and for different reasons.

In other words, diversity was organized differently in the two settlements. It would have been much more apparent in any district in Tenochtitlán than in Cuzco or one of the surrounding settlements. The effect of this was that peoples with very different backgrounds had more opportunity for face to face dealings with each other in the Aztec capital because of the internal structure of the settlement. This, of course, increased the possibilities for innovations to occur.

THE GROWTH AND DECLINE OF SETTLEMENTS

We have already indicated that archaeologists have been inordinately fond of studying towns and cities. So far, they have focused their attention on where these settlements occur when and how they emerged in the different areas, how they grew in size, and what effects they had on the populations that lived in the areas around them.

Traditions of living in year-round nucleated settlements appeared at various times in different parts of the New World. They were not confined exclusively to Mexico and Guatemala or to the Andean area between Colombia and northern Argentina and

Chile. They also occurred in the Amazonian rain forest, the American Southwest, and New England, to name only a few other regions where they were found. Some of these settlements were occupied for long periods of time; others were inhabited only briefly before they were abandoned. Some grew in size as the number of people residing in them increased; others never grew at all and remained much the same size throughout their existence.

In the face of changing social and economic conditions, we cannot satisfactorily explain the continuing existence or growth of some settlements in terms of their location alone. Nor can we adequately account for their continuity or expansion by referring solely to external factors—such as climatic change, warfare, and so forth. Instead, we must focus our attention on what was happening within the settlements themselves and on the social and economic conditions they were generating. This is important, because, up to this point, we have largely focused on external factors affecting settlements.

Settlements may start growing when their inhabitants add new kinds of work to the tasks they are already performing. This means that they are carrying out a greater variety and number of activities, requiring an increased division of labor. Let us consider how this process takes place and some of its consequences. First, we will summarize briefly the rise and fall of Teotihuacán, Mexico, and then examine in more detail the way in which new work is added to old. Teotihuacán is a gigantic archaeological site covering more than nine square miles which is located about twenty-five miles north of Mexico City. It was one of the largest preindustrial cities in the world, and, at the time of its greatest extent, between A.D. 450 and 650, it had a population of about 120,000 persons. For more than five hundred years, the city was a major cultural, economic, political, and religious center that influenced the course of events in virtually every part of Mesoamerica.

The Rise and Fall of Teotihuacán

During the first millennium B.C., the inhabitants of the Teotihuacán Valley exported obsidian and probably other commodities to groups living in other parts of Mesoamerica. During this period, the *teotihuacanos* were only one of several groups in Mesoamerica—and probably not even the most important one—that were exporting obsidian for making stone tools and ornaments. By the end of the first century B.C., the two settlements located at the site of Teotihuacán itself had already become the largest and probably the most important ones in the valley. They covered an area of about one and a half square miles and were inhabited by perhaps as many as 7500 persons. The goods sent to other parts of Mesoamerica presumably left the Teotihuacán Valley from the workshops and markets of these twin settlements.

The two settlements eventually merged into one covering an area of about six and a half square miles during the first century and a half of the Christian Era. By A.D. 150, Teotihuacán was already the largest and most imposing settlement in the area around the Valley of Mexico. Massive public construction occurred at the site during this 150-year period. The major north-south and east-west avenues that form the axis of the city were laid out, and the Pyramid of the Sun—the largest man-made structure in the New World—and probably the Pyramid of the Moon as well were built toward the end of this period. An estimated 45,000 persons lived in the city at this time, and perhaps an equal number resided in hamlets and small villages on the hill slopes overlooking the floor of the Teotihuacán Valley.

The city expanded to its greatest geographical extent—nearly nine square miles—during the next century, and its population rose to about 65,000 persons by A.D. 250. The *teotihuacanos* established close relationships with the Tajín peoples of the Gulf Coast region during this period, judging by the large number of features that appear in the city for the first time that seem to have their antecedents in that lowland region. The presence of Teotihuacán obsidian in places as far away as British Honduras suggests that the population was also becoming an increasingly important economic force in Mesoamerica.

The city grew explosively during the next two centuries, and by A.D. 450, its population was about 100,000 persons, who lived in the more than 4000 single-story apartment houses throughout the city. Surface remains around these apartment houses suggest that individuals who practiced the same craft—potters, weavers, stoneworkers, and featherworkers, to name only a few of the work activities performed in the city—lived in the same neighborhoods. At the same time, Teotihuacán's sphere of influence was increasing. It now included the highlands of Oaxaca and the Maya area as well as the Gulf Coast region.

Teotihuacán continued to grow after this time, although at a slower rate than it had before. The maximum population of the city—about 120,000 persons—was reached sometime during the period from A.D. 450 to 650, when it was the capital of an empire that included most of Mesoamerica. During this period, the *teotihuacanos* exported a wide range of goods and services—featherwork, obsidian, finished stone objects, several kinds of pottery, religion, and presumably soldiers and bureaucrats to administer the newly incorporated areas of the state. At the same time, they were importing a wide variety of goods—

such as feathers, cacao, jade, and probably certain kinds of agricultural produce that they could not grow locally.

Teotihuacán's influence began to wane after A.D. 650, and its population fell to about 100,000 persons during the next century. Its sphere of influence also diminished considerably from the preceding period, as new areas and communities began to emerge as increasingly important social and economic forces. Teotihuacán society collapsed completely after A.D. 750, and no more than 7500 persons lived in the ruins of the former metropolis during the next fifty years. Their influence, which had once extended throughout all of Mesoamerica, was now largely confined to the Teotihuacán Valley itself. Eventually, they were incorporated into a community from the north or replaced by members of this group.

The fall of Teotihuacán is certainly much more impressive or spectacular than the growth of the city because of the rapidity with which it occurred. It is probably also more difficult to explain. However, if we focus our attention on what was happening during the period of explosive population growth between A.D. 250 and 450 and compare it with what seems to have happened later, we may be able to shed some light on the city's collapse. The rapid growth of Teotihuacán after A.D. 250 was at least partly the result of what was happening to its industries and export economy. As an example of what was taking place, let us examine the obsidian industry, which was an important activity but certainly not the most important one in the city.

The Obsidian Industry

Surface remains found around obsidian workshops dating to different periods in the city's history tell us five facts about this industry. First, craftsmen who produced the same kinds of objects tended to live in the same neighborhoods. For instance, the artisans who made cores and blades lived in one part of the city, while those who specialized in the manufacture of arrowheads and dart points or various kinds of ornaments lived in other parts of the city. Second, the industry became increasingly specialized with the passage of time. The early craftsmen produced a wide range of goods. Eventually, some of them began to specialize in the production of cores and blades and, later, in the manufacture of projectile points and ceremonial or decorative objects. Third, there was a major technological innovation in the manufacture of cores and blades—the adoption of a particular way of preparing cores—that allowed the craftsmen specializing in this activity to produce a greater number of prismatic blades from a single core than they could earlier. Furthermore, these prismatic blades were more uniform in size and appearance than the ones produced by the older technique. Fourth, the craftsmen in general, but particularly those involved in the production of cores and blades, began to use more and more obsidian from areas outside of the Teotihuacán Valley. And, finally, the number of obsidian workshops in the city virtually tripled between A.D. 300 and 400.

The obsidian industry is an excellent example of how new work is added to old work. This new work was not added indiscriminately to the existing work activities; instead, it was added to specific parts of the older work. The *teotihuacanos* added the preparation of cores and blades to obsidian collecting. Once this became an established work activity in its own right, new kinds of work—the production of arrowheads and ornaments—were eventually added to it. The result of this process was increasing specialization and more division of labor in the community. The older work activities of the obsidian industry did not become obsolete as a result of the increased specialization. In fact, there seems to have been an even greater demand for unworked obsidian and for blades after arrowhead and ornament production became established craft specialities. The effect of this process was that a continually increasing number of people became involved in one aspect or another of the industry.

Most of the obsidian collected in the Teotihuacán Valley during the earlier periods in the city's history was apparently used locally for the production of tools and ornaments. The small portion that was exported probably consisted mainly of the unworked material. However, after the beginning of the Christian Era, two new factors affected the export economy. One was that the *teotihuacanos* began exporting obsidian to new areas—first to the highlands of Oaxaca and then to the Maya area. The second was that some of the craftsmen who formerly produced objects for local consumption began to export their finished goods to these new markets. Eventually, the exportation of finished objects became much more extensive and important to the city's economy than the exportation of unworked obsidian.

When the exports of Teotihuacán increased, the local economy of the city also grew. As the volume of the obsidian exports increased, more and more individuals became engaged in one aspect or another of the industry. Some of them worked as craftsmen in the workshops; others worked in the quarries in order to meet the growing needs of the craftsmen for more obsidian and for different kinds of obsidian; and still others were probably employed in exporting the finished products to distant markets. Each of the new jobs created by the increased demand for Teotihuacán obsidian added still other jobs to the city's economy. More and more individuals had to be employed in one way or another to meet the needs and demands of the growing numbers of obsidian workers.

As the export economy of the city grew, the *teotihuacanos* began to import a greater quantity and variety of goods from other areas. These imports also added to the local economy of the city. Some of the new imports—such as obsidian quarried outside of the valley—went directly into the growing export work. Other imports—such as pottery from the highlands of Oaxaca or the Maya area—were apparently used by the growing population of the city. In fact, after A.D. 400, there was at least one neighborhood in the city that was inhabited largely by peoples from Oaxaca. These foreigners were presumably involved in one way or another with the growing volume of imported goods that came into the city. They too must have added jobs to the local economy.

The Economy of Urban Growth

The information about Teotihuacán and its obsidian industry allows us to construct a two-stage model describing the process of urban growth. During the first stage, an export multiplier effect occurs, as groups that originally produced goods or performed services for local consumption begin to export some of their work. This adds to both the quantity and variety of the city's exports. Since the value of the goods and services leaving the settlement is greater, its residents can now afford to import a greater volume and range of products than they did earlier. Some of the additional imports—the unworked obsidian brought into Teotihuacán, for example—feed directly back into the export work of the city, while the rest are used or consumed locally. The goods and services provided by local producers also grow and diversify in order to meet the increased needs of the groups who are now exporting new products. The new jobs and kinds of work that are available provide a stimulus for population growth by attracting people from the surrounding area. The goods and services used locally continue to increase and diversify even further because of the growth of the settlement's population.

The export multiplier effect does not occur at a fixed rate. Instead, it may vary considerably from one settlement to another and from one period to the next in the history of the same settlement. The export multiplier effect is higher when one or more of the following conditions prevail: (1) the proportion of raw materials imported is larger than that of finished goods; (2) a larger proportion of the imports goes directly back into local production than goes to local consumption; (3) the number of local producers supplying goods and services to the producers of exports is large; and (4) these local producers are independent of the exporting groups.

A settlement like Teotihuacán grows gradually but steadily when its inhabitants are generating new exports from the local economy. As a result, they acquire a considerable quantity and variety of imports. The second stage of the growth process— probably more important than the export multiplier effect in the long run—begins to operate when the inhabitants of the settlement replace some of the finished goods they import with locally manufactured products. Before this process can occur, however, two conditions must exist in the settlement. There must be a sufficient demand, or market, for some of the imported goods so that it is economically feasible for someone in the settlement to begin producing them locally. Furthermore, the inhabitants of the settlement must have the technical capabilities to manufacture or produce these goods by adding new work activities to the ones they are already performing. This process is called the import replacement effect.

Let us examine how the import replacement effect might have operated in Teotihuacán and what consequences it would have had on the city's economy. The *teotihuacanos* probably imported a great quantity and variety of goods, some of which were durable items—precious stones, obsidian, and pottery—that have been preserved in the archaeological record, but most of which probably consisted of perishable commodities—feathers, food-stuffs, and rubber—that were either completely consumed or not preserved because of the soil conditions that exist at the site. Consequently, it is difficult to determine exactly which imports were replaced with locally manufactured goods and when this happened. However, it is clear that the process had occurred many times by the middle of the third century A.D. Jade masks from western Mexico were undoubtedly only one of the imports replaced during this period. By A.D. 250, the stoneworking industries of Teotihuacán had become very specialized, and the city already had the technical capacity to make stone masks. As the demand for jade masks increased, it became profitable for some of the stoneworkers to produce them locally.

When this happened, the *teotihuacanos* were increasing the size of their local economy by adding new jobs to it. One of the consequences of producing the masks locally was that there were probably more of them available than there had been earlier. More important than this, however, was the fact that jade masks no longer had to be imported from the peoples of western Mexico and paid for with exported goods. As a result, the *teotihuacanos* could change the composition of their imports and shift to other goods and services, without expanding the size of their export economy. Some of the new imports—such as unworked jade—were probably incorporated immediately into the locally produced goods and services that had been imported in the past. The rest of the new imports were extras in the sense that they consisted either of greater quantities of the items that the residents of the city were continuing to import or of new items that had not been imported earlier. From the *teotihuacanos'* perspective, it probably seemed that the volume of their imports was increasing. They had all of the goods they had had earlier and more of some of them. And, they had some new items that had not been available earlier because of the shift in the composition of their imports.

Import replacement created new jobs in the local economy. Some of the new jobs were directly involved in producing the goods and services formerly imported. However, each of these added still more jobs to the local economy, for an increasing number of individuals had to be employed to meet the growing needs and demands of the new producers. Since the *teotihuacanos* probably replaced a number of imports about the same time, the number of new jobs available increased rapidly. As a result, the population of the city grew, and the markets for each of the items now being produced locally were considerably larger than they had been earlier.

The import replacement effect has a number of consequences. Growth occurs in the local economy without an increase in the volume of either the imports or the exports of a settlement. Furthermore, both the quantity and variety of the goods and services that are being produced by the community have increased considerably. This sets up a situation where the members of the community can generate new exports from the local economy. If the exports of the community are growing at the same time its members are replacing imported items with locally produced ones, then the imports will not only change in composition but also increase in volume. This can lead to a positive feedback situation where very rapid economic growth is possible. Judging by the continuous growth of Teotihuacán's population, this is apparently what was happening in the city from its inception to the period between A.D. 450 and 650.

Teotihuacán influence waned rapidly after A.D. 650. There are many explanations for its decline. Some focus on what was happening in the city and its environs, while others focus on what was taking place outside of this area. First, the rural sustaining areas could no longer support the city's population. Food was becoming scarcer because of drought, erosion of agricultural land as a result of local deforestation for fuel and building materials, and the inability of foot porters to meet the growing demands of the city's population by carrying food from more distant localities. This produced food shortages in the city, probably reducing the nutritional levels of the lower classes and eventually leading to a decline in population as some residents emigrated to other localities where food was more easily obtained. Second, the depopulation of the city reduced the size of its labor force and, ultimately, must have produced manpower shortages in its export industries. As the understaffed workshops produced continually smaller quantities of export goods, the quantity and variety of imported goods appearing in the city's markets declined and the process of replacing imported goods and services with locally produced ones eventually ground to a stop. Third, communities that traded almost exclusively with Teotihuacán between A.D. 450 and 650 began to trade more extensively with other groups after this period. This is particularly evident in the Maya area, where there were increased contacts between the communities of the Guatemala lowlands, British Honduras, the Yucatan Peninsula, and the Gulf Coast region after about A.D. 600. As these new exchange networks were established, Teotihuacán lost markets for its goods, and the volume of its imports and exports declined even further. Eventually, these other groups rivaled Teotihuacán, and ultimately one of them—a group from the north called the Toltecs—became the most important social and economic force in the area.

THE TOWN AND ITS REGION

The activities—food production, industry, commerce, and the various broadly defined services mentioned earlier—by which groups sustain themselves do not necessarily have to be carried out in the same locality. But at various times and places in ancient America, groups chose to perform several of them in the same place. This decision often resulted in the formation of nucleated settlements called towns or cities. Where the majority of the population lived in the nucleated settlements and the rural areas between them were largely uninhabited, there may have been a clear distinction between town and countryside. Where a significant portion of the population lived in the rural areas, the distinction between town and countryside may have been less clear, for the two appeared to blend gradually into each other. In either situation, however, it is impossible to divorce the town from the region around it.

There is a region around each town that exists in symbiosis with it. The townspeople depend on the region for most of their food and raw materials. They may provide these resources themselves through control of the rural lands, or the rural population may be organized to provide the products for the townspeople. For the rural population of the region, the town may be an employment center, a collecting and distributing point for their products, and a marketing center for goods and services that come from outside the immediate area. It may also be a meeting place and cultural center—a focal point of social life and a clearinghouse of information. The townspeople thus provide goods and services for the rural population of the region. The mechanism integrating town and region is the movement toward the town and away from it—centripedal and centrifugal—of people, goods, and services.

Towns create food-producing districts around them even when some of their residents maintain small gardens within the limits of the settlement. Some foods—such as corn or beans—can be stored fairly easily and do not have to be consumed as soon as they ripen. These foods can be brought to the town from considerable distances. More perishable foods—particularly fruits like avocados—must be consumed almost as soon as they ripen. Consequently, they must be brought into the town almost daily. The differential preservation of various foods, as well as differences in the amounts of care that they require, often leads to roughly concentric zones of food resources around the town. The perishable foods or the ones requiring a great deal of care may be grown closest to the settlement. Those that are easily stored, travel well, or require relatively little care can be grown farther away from the town. The needs of the townspeople shape not only the kinds of food-producing activities that take place in the region but also their distribution in it.

By drawing raw materials from the countryside, the town creates rural sustaining areas for its industries and can provide labor or employment for some segment of the regional population. These sustaining areas do not have to correspond in size and shape to the town's food-producing district, for the townspeople may draw raw materials for their industries from much greater distances than their food supply. For example, it is unlikely that the inhabitants of Teotihuacán ever drew much of their food from outside of the Valley of Mexico; however, they were regularly acquiring unworked obsidian from Pachuca, nearly fifty miles north.

Towns can generate the development of home or cottage industries in the regions around them because of their collecting and marketing facilities. The townspeople can pass on the raw materials they acquire from outside of the immediate area to the rural population around them and then collect the finished products from these groups. Such rural industries are usually in the immediate vicinity of the towns.

Towns also create recruitment areas in the surrounding regions. Their size varies from one town to another, reflecting not only the town's power of attraction but also the network of communication with the surrounding countryside. Rural people—hearing of work or other opportunities available in the towns—often move into them to take advantage of what they have to offer. A town's power of attraction also depends to some extent on its size and whether or not its economy is growing. For example, the recruitment area of Teotihuacán was much greater during the fifth century when its population and economy were growing steadily than it was after the city's influence began to wane after about A.D. 650. A town's power of attraction does not always have to be based on fact; rural peoples can have an illusion about what is available in the town, and this image can be just as effective a magnet as real opportunities.

The main significance of towns to the rural populations around them lies in the goods and services they can provide. If access to these goods and services is localized in the town, then the rural peoples must come into the settlement to acquire them; if access is controlled by the townspeople but not centralized in the settlement, then some segment of the urban group may travel into the countryside to peddle their wares. Both patterns of influence could exist simultaneously in the same region. The distances that these goods or services will move through the town's region will vary from one item to another. For example, the zone influenced by a famous shrine—perhaps one like the Temple of the Sun at Teotihuacán—was undoubtedly much more extensive than the zones influenced by individual craftsmen or small merchants living in the city.

Urban geographers have recognized the gradient character of a town's influence. They distinguish three areas of influence in a town region. First is the area that has direct, daily communication with the town. The population of this area maintains the closest ties with the townspeople. Second is the area that has occasional communications with the town. The population of this area maintains permanent ties with the townspeople but deals with them less frequently than the inhabitants of the first area. The population of the third area has very infrequent communication with the townspeople—for example, its members visit the town only once or twice a year to attend or participate in some sort of special activity. The town's influence is expressed in a much less regular way in this area.

The extent of a town's influence depends in part on the number of other towns in the area. The most important town in such an area is usually the one with the greatest population or the largest number of facilities. The inhabitants of each town region in the area rely on the facilities offered by the major center of their region; for what it lacks, they must rely on another town. The result may be a hierarchy of towns. Each town is the center of a region, with the hamlets and villages of that region as its satellites. At the same time, however, the town may be one of the satellites of a larger, more influential center that dominates the area as a whole.

The extent of a town's influence can change considerably with the passage of time, for the links that bind it to the surrounding area are dynamic ones that reflect the appearance of new social and economic conditions. In the remainder of this section, let us consider briefly the impact of the rise and fall of Teotihuacán on the inhabitants of the area around it. As the reader will recall, Teotihuacán is located in a relatively small valley that drains into the northeastern corner of the Valley of Mexico. Until fairly recent times, the floor of the Valley of Mexico was covered by a chain of large, shallow lakes, so that the ancient settlements of the area are concentrated along the edges of the basin, which is roughly seventy-five miles long and forty-five miles wide.

When the twin settlements appeared at Teotihuacán during the first century B.C., other towns on the eastern and southern edges of the Valley of Mexico rivaled or surpassed them in both size and population. Each of the large towns that have been discovered in this area—Teotihuacán, El Tepalcate, Tlapacoyán, and Cuicuilco, proceeding southward around the lake—may have been the centers of town regions roughly twenty miles in diameter, in each of which there were satellite settlements. The largest of the towns in the Valley of Mexico, and probably the most important one judging by its large public buildings, was Cuicuilco. The relative homogeneity of the ceramic assemblages in the regions along the eastern and southern edges of the basin suggests that all of them participated to a considerable extent in the same economic sphere. This does not mean, of course, that the relationships between them were amicable. They may not have been, for the populations could have been competing with each other for access to the same resources and control of trade routes.

Major changes occurred in the valley as Teotihuacán gradually acquired dominance during the first century and a half of the Christian Era. The rural population, at least along its eastern edge, and perhaps along the southern one as well, was much smaller than it had been earlier. The major towns of the preceding period were also depopulated and had many fewer residents than they had previously. Several conclusions can be drawn from this evidence. First, many people whose ancestors had lived elsewhere in the valley were now being attracted to Teotihuacán because of the goods, services, and opportunities it offered. Second, the other towns in the valley gradually became satellites of Teotihuacán. Third, the regions associated with these towns may have been about the same size as they were earlier, but the links between the townspeople and their rural populations were

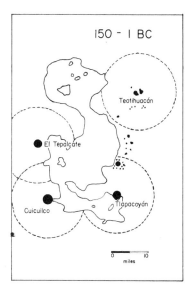
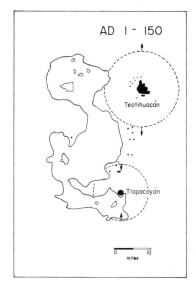
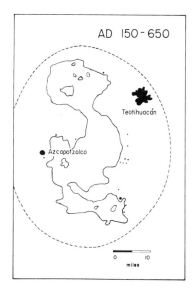
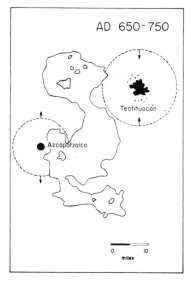

Fig. 4–4. Changes in the extent of Teotihuácan influence in the Valley of Mexico and the location of settlements in different periods. Archaeological investigations have been much more intensive on the eastern side of the lake between Teotihuácan and Tlapacoyán than they have on the western side of the lake.

much weaker. The towns could no longer furnish what they had provided earlier, because the *teotihuacanos* gradually took over these functions.

Many of the processes that began in the Valley of Mexico during the first century A.D. continued to operate well into the seventh century. The growth of Teotihuacán was accompanied by a progressive decline in the rural proportion of the total population. A large segment of the rural population moved either to Teotihuacán or to one of the small nucleated settlements that were attached socially, politically, and economically to it. Judging by the relative scarcity of archaeological sites dating from this period elsewhere in central Mexico—particularly western Puebla, Tlaxcala, and Morelos—and the clear evidence of Teotihuacán influence in the ones that are known, the city probably attracted part of its growing population from areas outside of the basin itself. In other words, the recruitment area of Teotihuacán expanded enormously after the fourth century.

New areas and peoples were incorporated into Teotihuacán's sphere of influence, which now included not only the Valley of Mexico but also areas lying outside of the basin as well. The small, nucleated settlements that were contemporary with the city may have been provincial administrative centers which served as collecting points for goods that were eventually sent to the metropolis. The populations of the town regions associated with these centers were probably becoming increasingly dependent on Teotihuacán for many of the goods and services they needed. Some of the rural communities around the lakes apparently exploited almost exclusively a single resource: they produced salt, collected aquatic plants and insects, or hunted the migratory birds that gathered around the lakes. The existence of these highly specialized communities suggests that the links binding their residents to the townspeople of their region may have been fewer and weaker than they had been earlier.

Other inferences can also be drawn about Teotihuacán's impact on the surrounding areas during this period. The relative depopulation of rural areas in the Valley of Mexico suggests that the residents of Teotihuacán may have controlled or owned more rural land than they had earlier. There was probably increased productivity in the food-producing districts located around the city. This could have been accomplished by enlarging the fields, intensifying existing food production techniques, or a combination of both. There was probably also a significant expansion in the size of the rural sustaining areas for the city's industries.

It appears that the entire rural population of the Teotihuacán Valley moved into the city between A.D. 650 and 750; however, even this did not check the decline of the city's population as a whole. At the same time, the provincial administrative centers of the preceding period—such as Atzcaputzalco on the west side of the Valley of Mexico—were growing. Some of the population that left Teotihuacán probably returned to these settlements and their environs. Judging by the differences between the ceramics of these centers and those of the city itself, the former were apparently in the process of acquiring some degree of economic independence from the *teotihuacanos*. This process might have been fostered by the kind of economic overspecialization that appeared in the Valley of Mexico during the preceding period when Teotihuacán ruled all of Mesoamerica and entire communities in the basin seem to have devoted their energies to exploiting a single resource area or producing a single commodity.

As Teotihuacán's sphere of influence began to diminish, the city was no longer recruiting people from either the Valley of Mexico or areas outside of it. Instead, it began to lose population to centers that were emerging in these areas. This process was probably accompanied by a reduction in the size of the city's food-producing districts and the rural sustaining areas for its industries. At the same time, other town regions in the Valley of Mexico and its environs were becoming increasingly independent of what was happening in the city and more important as social and economic forces in the area.

After Teotihuacán society collapsed completely, most of the population returned to small towns and villages that were located around the edges of the Valley of Mexico. Within the basin, these towns were undoubtedly just as important and influential as Teotihuacán; however, they were to come increasingly under the influence of regional power centers that were emerging outside of the Valley of Mexico at Tula to the north, Xochicalco to the south, and Cholula to the southeast. Eventually, the center at Tula—the Toltec capital—became the dominant social and economic force in northern Mesoamerica, while Teotihuacán and the Valley of Mexico became a cultural and political backwash.

The town can exert a powerful influence over what happens in the area around it by altering the traditional social and economic patterns of the rural population. It is clear from the central Mexican evidence that urbanism is never imposed uniformly over an entire area; instead, the people of a region tend to concentrate where they can best satisfy their needs. This may be in the center of a region or in one of the small settlements linked to it. The central Mexican data, as well as those from other areas, suggest that urbanization is not an inevitable process. From a regional perspective at least, it is a reversible one. Urban settlements emerge in an area when certain social and economic conditions prevail and disappear when these conditions no longer favor their continued existence.

5. Native American States

Every ethnic group has some kind of political organization. It may be very apparent in those groups where there are formal officers, large bureaucracies, or marked differences in wealth, power, and status between the rulers and the ruled. Political organization may be less obvious in others where these features do not occur but where, nevertheless, there are still mechanisms for determining which individuals or groups should be listened to in given situations. Many kinds of political organizations existed among the native peoples of the New World. Even in the central Andes, which is often viewed as a relatively homogeneous area, there was great variation. For example, before the Inca conquest, some ethnic groups in the Andean area had highly centralized governments with hereditary rulers and elite groups, while others apparently lacked any kind of centralized political authority.

POLITICAL ORGANIZATION AND THE STATE

In recent years, there has been considerable debate over the relationship between political organization and the nature of the state. Some writers argue that the two are coterminous. Where there is political organization, there is a state. Other writers have argued that the state is a particular kind of political organization—one characterized by social stratification, differential access to basic resources, obedience to government officials, institutionalized sanctions based on force, or the willingness to defend a particular territory. Some writers want to get rid of the concept of the state altogether, while to others it retains a certain utility from their perspective.

At various times and places in the Americas, one ethnic group has exercised some degree of control over the actions and affairs of its neighbors. For the purposes of this discussion, these political units composed of more than one ethnic group are states. This definition of the state does not describe how control was exerted by one group over another or even what form it took. It merely says that several formerly autonomous groups became linked into some kind of dominant-subordinate relationship with each other.

Let us look a little closer at these dominant-subordinate relationships before examining the archaeological evidence for existence of a state. The dominant ethnic group in a state does not impinge uniformly on all of the aspects of behavior of the subordinate groups. It affects certain sectors of their behavior and leaves the others relatively untouched. As a result, the subordinate groups are linked to the dominant one in those sectors where they interact with it. They adjust their behavior in these respects to the standards of the dominant group. The rest of their behavior is relatively insulated from the standards of the dominant group. In other words, the members of a subordinate group may have to provide land and labor to the governing group, but the rulers do not tell them what kinds of clothes they should wear, what kinds of houses they should build, or what kinds of pottery they should use. The demands imposed by the dominant group can vary considerably from one situation to another and reflect the principles by which its members have organized their state.

From an archaeological perspective, it may be easier to recognize the process of state formation than the existence of a state itself. It is not hard to discern autonomous ethnic groups and their boundaries from the archaeological record. The members of one group live in certain kinds of houses, use certain kinds of pottery, or bury their dead in certain ways. In general, they leave particular patterns of archaeological evidence that distinguish them from other contemporary groups. As a result, it is not too difficult to determine that the Moche group, for example, occupied this valley at A.D. 450, while the Nasca one occupied that valley at the same time.

However, what is happening when we see some of the distinctive archaeological patterns associated with one ethnic group suddenly appear in community territories where they never occurred before? It may reflect nothing more than the flow of prestige from one group to another or the establishment of some sort of exchange relationship between them. But it may also represent the formation of a state. Do the archaeological patterns associated with the donor group spread rapidly? Are these patterns imposed uniformly in all of the recipient groups? Do they produce massive changes in the archaeological patterns of the recipient groups? Does the donor group establish specialized settlements—such as storehouses, garrisons, or administrative centers—in the territories of the recipients? Is there any evidence of warfare associated with the spread of the donor group? If the answers to these and similar questions are yes, then we may well be witnessing the formation of a state in the archaeological record.

When the Europeans first came to the Americas, they were impressed by the kinds of political organizations they found in the central Andes, Mexico, and parts of Colombia, because they were similar, superficially at least, to their own. In each of these areas, large numbers of ethnic groups had been incorporated into states that were dominated by one group. The subordinate groups were generally linked to the dominant ones by political and economic ties; however, the particular form of these linkages varied considerably from one area to another. Although interesting in itself, this variation represents something more important.

In each of the areas, many ethnic groups shared the same idea about how they should organize their activities to acquire the resources they needed. In one area, the idea was that the ethnic group should have access to and control of all the required resources. In another, it was that the ethnic group should trade with neighboring peoples for items that could not be acquired or produced locally. These ideas reflect the different ecological patterns and resource distributions in each of the areas. In the central Andes and Mesoamerica—two areas where the archaeology is fairly well known—the ideas may have considerable antiquity, and they served as organizing principles for the states that appeared there. In the sections that follow, let us examine in more detail how these principles were applied and some of their implications.

STATE FORMATION IN THE CENTRAL ANDES

A widespread form of social organization in the central Andes is one of community self-sufficiency. Ideally, this means each ethnic group controls all of the resources it needs to sustain itself throughout the year. As a result, its members do not have to rely on other groups to provide essential goods and services. The most important consequence of this form of organization is that the members of a group must space themselves efficiently throughout their territory to acquire their resources.

The Andean Pattern: Community Self-Sufficiency

These group territories are superimposed on a diverse environment characterized by a wide variety of food resources, each with its own ecological requirements. Consequently, there are local differences in the occurrence and abundance of these resources. There are seasonal and often annual variations in the availability of many of them, particularly those that live in terrestrial habitats. The central Andean environment is an exceedingly complex mosaic produced by systematic differences in elevation, temperature, and the availability of water, to name only a few of the more obvious variables involved. Let us consider the ecological patterns and, more importantly, the patterns of resource distribution in the area.

For our purposes, there are two important patterns in the environmental diversity. One pattern is repetitive, and the other is linear. The repetitive pattern consists of a series of ecological habitats and resource areas that repeats itself every ten to twenty miles. It is most apparent on the Peruvian coast as one moves from one river valley to the next at roughly the same elevation; however, it also occurs in the highlands as one travels from one river valley across the *puna* to the next. The linear pattern involves a sequence of habitats and resource areas that never repeats itself. Again, this pattern is perhaps most clearly expressed on the west side of the Andes where one moves very quickly from sea level to the crest of the western mountain range which varies between about 16,000 and 20,000 feet in elevation. This pattern is also characteristic of every river valley in the highlands, even though it is not so obvious because the elevation gradients are less pronounced in this region.

The distinction between repetitive and linear arrangements of resource areas had important implications concerning where people went to get their food. The food immediately available to a population living on the coast near the mouth of a river was roughly the same as that available to populations in similar settings in other coastal valleys, but very different from the food immediately available to populations in the middle or upper parts of the same river valley. If the coastal population sought new resources its members would be more likely to find them in the higher parts of their own valley than north or south along the coast. If the local supply of a particular resource was inadequate for this population, then its members would probably be most successful in finding additional sources of it in similar environments in the valleys located immediately to the north or south.

The ideal of community self-sufficiency is probably an ancient one in the central Andes. We find suggestions of it on the central coast of Peru nearly 7000 years ago. A group living in the lower part of the Lurín Valley maintained a year-round settlement in the same place, and its members exploited the seasonally and permanently available foods of several contiguous resource areas close to their village. A neighboring group fifty miles to the north in the Ancón-Chillón region exploited essentially the same re-

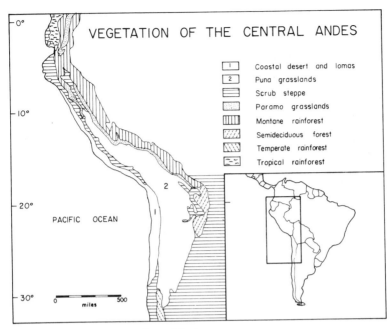

Fig. 5-1. Vegetation of the Central Andes.

sources but was not able to maintain year-round settlements because of the spacing of resource areas in its territory. The members of this group moved from one locality to another as the seasonal food resources of each place became available. Although both groups were obviously in contact with neighboring ones—judging by the widespread similarities in the kinds of stone tools that were being made in Peru at that time—neither of them seems to have depended on other peoples for the food they used.

This pattern of community self-sufficiency gradually broke down on the central Peruvian coast after about 2500 B.C. in the face of population growth and the emergence of a new economic orientation in the area. A new pattern of self-sufficiency appeared based on the exchange of foodstuffs between members of the same community who lived in different parts of the communal territory and intensively utilized the resources immediately around their settlements. Some of these populations fished and collected shellfish along the coast, while others farmed in the lower and middle parts of the coastal river valleys. The inhabitants of the fishing villages made marine protein foods available to the inland populations and received agricultural produce in return.

At first, these exchange systems operated over relatively short distances—perhaps a day's walk or less—between the large fishing villages that were frequently located outside of the river

95

valleys and the small farming hamlets that were located in the valleys. The distribution of large archaeological sites between 2500 and 1900 B.C. suggests that the availability of marine protein foods rather than agricultural produce played the major role in determining the location, permanency, and size of settlements. However, as cultivated plant foods gradually became more important after 1900 B.C., an increasing proportion of the population became involved in agricultural production around the settlements in the river valleys. These settlements were separated from each other by as much as a three- or four-day walk. The exchange networks that operated after 1900 B.C. are distinguished from the earlier ones by the greater number of settlements that participated in the system, the greater travel distances involved between settlements located at opposite ends of the system, and the greater quantity and variety of goods that were moved from one settlement to another.

Although evidence is scarce from the Andean highlands, analogous patterns of community self-sufficiency probably prevailed in this area as well. Data from Ayacucho suggest that the early inhabitants of this region moved from one place to another throughout the year as the seasonal resources of each locality became available. After about 2500 B.C., they seem to have settled in or near different resource areas with the bulk of the population concentrated where agriculture could be practiced. Presumably, foodstuffs were also exchanged between the various settlements that made up the Ayacucho ethnic group at that time.

These communal exchange systems were apparently organized around a river valley and the adjacent coastal or mountainous areas. Several autonomous ethnic groups may have occupied different parts of the long, low-gradient river valleys in the highlands. On the coast, there may have been a separate ethnic group in each river valley after 1900 B.C. The evidence for this consists of intervalley differences in the kinds of contemporary archaeological assemblages that have been found. Some of these differences were relatively minor matters of style and technique—for instance, the ways in which textiles were made and decorated or the steps involved in making a shell fishhook. Other differences involved the patterns of archaeological associations that occurred or did not occur in particular valleys. For example, caches of tools, textiles, and food have been found in the area immediately north of the Chillón Valley, but they have not been found in this valley or south of it. These exchange systems, generally organized around a single valley, efficiently utilized the environmental diversity and ecological patterning of the Andes.

If we looked at the Andean area as it was about 1500 B.C., three other patterns, besides community self-sufficiency, would stand out. First, agricultural production—probably involving various water management techniques, such as small irrigation canals in some of the coastal valleys—had enormously expanded the carrying capacities of the environments in many regions. These new perceptions of the environments and ways of exploiting them facilitated extensive population growth over long periods of time. The population growth rates associated with these new economic orientations were probably relatively low—about 0.2 percent a year is one estimate for the central coast between 2500 and 1700 B.C.—and probably varied among regions and over time.

The second pattern was unequal social and economic development. Some of the autonomous groups had large populations and maintained large nucleated settlements that probably supported some degree of craft specialization and status differentiation. At the same time, the members of other groups either moved from place to place throughout the year or resided in relatively small nucleated settlements that were probably less socially and economically differentiated than the larger ones in other regions. This kind of social and economic variation reflects, among other things, differences in the agricultural potential of the various regions in the Andes; regions with high agricultural potentials could support large populations while those without sufficient natural endowments supported smaller populations.

The third pattern was that the various autonomous groups did not exist in isolation. Widespread similarities in architectural and pottery styles, for example, indicate that many of them were in close contact with each other. They were bound together by communication networks that crossed both the coastal desert and the *puna* grasslands and even breached the crest of the western mountain range in those places where relatively low passes existed. Each of the half dozen or so communication networks that existed in Peru between 1700 and 1000 B.C. incorporated communities from a number of different river valleys.

These communication networks reflected prestige relationships between the participating groups. Some communities were more influential than others, either because of their size or because of some special activity, product, or historical association that conferred prestige on them. Other groups participating in the same network often imitated the behavior of the more influential one in order to acquire some of its prestige as well as the beneficial good or service associated with it. They either borrowed the prestigious item directly or produced their own copies of it.

Perhaps the most important example of this process in the Andean area was the spread of the Chavin art style about 1000 B.C. Chavin art was associated with a religious cult in which oracles may have played a prominent role. The spread of the art style coincided with the spread of the cult along the major communication routes that connected large nucleated settlements and their satellites in much of northern and central Peru. There is no evidence at all that military conquest was involved in this expansion. In fact, the patterns of archaeological evidence associated with the spread of Chavin closely resemble those associated with the spread of early Christianity around the Mediterranean Basin or the expansion of Pachacamac influence, which was mentioned briefly in the last chapter.

Representations of Chavin mythical beings reappeared sporadically in the Andean area for more than 2000 years. This suggests that prestige can be transmitted through time as well as space. It also suggests that there may have been a continuous tradition of Chavin ideas in the area, although it would be difficult to prove this with the evidence that is now available. The spread of Chavin probably had very little to do with the formation of states in the Andean area during the first millennium B.C., but it may have provided a general model for at least part of what happened in later times.

Emergence of New Patterns in the Andes

A new pattern emerged in coastal Peru at least during the last half of the first millennium B.C. It consisted of five elements that appeared at different times in different places: (1) exchange networks that apparently incorporated the populations of several adjacent valleys, (2) fortified hilltop settlements in many regions, (3) burials containing individuals with no heads or individuals with their own heads as well as those of others tied around their waists, (4) occasional burials of individuals with massive depressed skull fractures or projectile points imbedded in vital areas of their bodies, and (5) the occurrence of stray bits and pieces of human bone in garbage dumps. This pattern is usually interpreted as one involving raiding, conquest, or some combination of both. The question we might ask now is what conditions would have precipitated the gradual appearance of this pattern.

Two things are fairly clear in the archaeological records of many parts of Peru toward the end of the first millennium B.C. First, agricultural practices at this time were probably not much more intensive than they had been 1500 years earlier, although new domesticated plant foods had been added to the daily diets of many communities, and perhaps more of their territories were under cultivation. Second, the populations of many coastal valleys were significantly larger at the beginning of the Christian Era than 1500 years before. If we assume a steady but low population growth rate—on the order of 0.23 percent a year—then the total population of an area like Ancón-Chillón would have risen from about 1500 to more than 47,000 persons between 1800 and 350 B.C. Even though the later estimate for Ancón-Chillón is too high because of our assumption, population changes of this magnitude do not contradict the available evidence from a number of coastal valleys.

The combination of these factors may have produced scarcities of some commodities. The food produced in some territories was not sufficient to sustain increased populations at culturally defined nutritional levels. This deficiency of foodstuffs would have acted as a brake on population growth in some of these ethnic groups. Instead of intensifying production some groups turned to other areas where these foods were available. Because of the ecological patterning in the Andes, such areas were neighboring valleys for coastal populations and adjacent valleys or neighboring parts of the same valley for highland groups. These areas were raided or conquered to acquire scarce resources; however, the items defined as scarce and desirable were not necessarily the same ones that were limiting population growth. The effect of their activities, whatever the motivations immediately underlying them, was that these groups probably acquired more of the foodstuffs they needed.

The multi-valley exchange networks that gradually appeared between 350 B.C. and A.D. 550 probably correspond closely with the boundaries of small independent states. The boundaries between these political units, as well as their size and number, fluctuated almost continuously throughout this period. At one moment, four or five valley populations may have belonged to the same unit. A few hundred years later, there may have been two political units in the same area, or the whole region may have been incorporated into an even larger political entity. The dominant-subordinate relationships between the various valley populations in one of these units also changed through time. At one moment, the population of one valley may have been the most important group in the unit, replaced a few hundred years later by the population of another valley. This, of course, tells us very little about the kinds of relationships that existed among the groups incorporated into a single state or the forms of government that prevailed. Judging by historical descriptions of the patterns that prevailed later, these must have been highly varied during this period.

A complex set of events occurred between A.D. 450 and 550 that had a considerable impact on what happened during the next two centuries. First, the total population seems to have reached some sort of maximum, at least in the coastal region. Evidence from Ancón-Chillón suggests that the total population of this area may have been as high as 60,000 persons, or roughly equivalent to what it was at the time of the Spanish conquest. Second, there was an interval of slightly increased rainfall in the highlands which resulted in slightly greater runoffs in the rivers of the coastal valleys. This opened up the possibility of farming in formerly marginal areas. Third, water control systems were expanded considerably in several coastal valleys to take advantage of the increased runoff and to bring marginal areas under cultivation.

Rainfall gradually returned to normal or even subnormal levels by about A.D. 450. Farming became increasingly difficult and then impossible in the marginal habitats. For instance, the people of the Ica Valley built an irrigation canal in one marginal area during the height of the wet period and grew a wide variety of crops in the region. As the amount of available river water diminished, they began to grow only those crops that were particularly well adapted to dry conditions. Eventually, they abandoned the area altogether when there was no longer enough water even for these crops. The total amount of land under cultivation probably began to diminish after about A.D. 500. The effects of such a reduction would have been felt most strongly in those areas where large amounts of marginal land can be brought under cultivation with only a slight increase in rainfall. This situation probably created population pressures of varying intensities on the existing food resources in some parts of the Andes.

The Huari Empire

The Lake Titicaca basin and Ayacucho were two regions affected by these drought conditions. As marginal lands became first difficult and then impossible to farm, the inhabitants of the two areas were presumably faced with food shortages. In order to eliminate these scarcities and, at the same time, maintain their self-sufficiency, they sought and acquired resources from other parts of the Andean area. Large multi-ethnic states emerged in both areas between A.D. 550 and 750. The smaller of the two was the Tiahuanaco Empire which had its capital at the southern end of Lake Titicaca. At its greatest extent, Tiahuanaco was larger than any of the earlier Andean states and included most of the Bolivian highlands as well as northern Chile and the southernmost part of Peru. The Huari Empire had its capital near Ayacucho and, by 750, included virtually all of the coastal and highland areas of Peru.

At the present time, we have much more information about the Huari Empire than Tiahuanaco, so let us focus our attention on it. Other ethnic groups were incorporated into the Huari state by military conquest in some instances, probably by threats and coercion in others, and by apparently peaceful acceptance of their rule in one case. The people of Huari maintained their self-sufficiency by organizing the groups they subjected into subordinate positions and by liberally helping themselves to their subjects' resources. Their territory now included most of Peru, and Huari received the additional food and other goods it needed by relying on the production of ethnic groups that lived in other areas. These groups continued to produce and consume largely on the basis of old regional patterns. The state was mainly concerned with collecting goods at Huari and the provincial administrative centers and with redistributing them when it was necessary—for example, to supply armies engaged in conquest or suppressing rebellions, to feed and clothe state officials, or to assist peoples in drought-stricken areas. Large numbers of people were needed to govern the empire. Higher officials probably belonged to the Huari ethnic group, while the others were drawn from the traditional elite sectors of the subject groups. These traditional elite groups must have had mixed loyalties. They served the state but belonged to the groups they governed and represented. In the long run, this practice probably undermined exactly what Huari was trying to create: a politically unified state in which all power and authority ultimately emanated from a small ruling class in Ayacucho.

The empire expanded rapidly between A.D. 600 and 650 and again between A.D. 700 and 750. Even though they had real economic reasons for establishing an empire, it appears that the people of Huari used their religion, as the Incas did later, as the means for justifying their conquests. They imposed this religion—one of the major figures of which was a new version of an old Chavin deity—on the ethnic groups incorporated into their state. From an economic perspective, the people of Huari main-

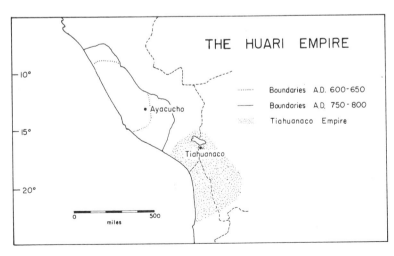

THE HUARI EMPIRE

.... Boundaries A.D. 600-650

———— Boundaries A.D. 750-800

Tiahuanaco Empire

10°

• Ayacucho

15°

Tiahuanaco

20°

0   500
    miles

Fig. 5–2. The Huari Empire.

tained their self-sufficiency by exporting a scarce commodity—their religion—and receiving land and other resources in return for these religious truths.

The empire collapsed suddenly after A.D. 750. The capital city was virtually abandoned, some coastal areas were depopulated, and, within a few centuries, small regional states appeared in various parts of the old empire. Let us examine two of the more obvious factors involved in the collapse of the Huari Empire. First, the demands of the state increased continually as the size of its bureaucracy grew. These demands were met, perhaps relatively easily, as long as the size of the state was increasing and new ethnic groups were incorporated into it. The additional goods and services required could be drawn from the newly incorporated areas of the empire. However, once the state stopped expanding geographically, the additional demands had to be met by groups already supplying Huari. This placed a continually increasing burden on these communities and must have been a source of growing dissatisfaction as they saw more and more of their produce and labor drawn off by the state. Second, there were few, if any, technological innovations during this period that significantly increased the productive capacities of the various local communities in the empire. Total production may actually have diminished after about A.D. 700 in the depopulated coastal areas because of manpower shortages; however, there is no evidence that the state responded to the plight of these communities by reducing the amount it demanded from them.

The difficulties and frustrations that must have accompanied the growing demands of the state may well have set the stage for revolutionary changes in the Huari Empire. It appears that the state was either unwilling or unable to rectify the problems it was creating. At the same time, it was unable to prevent changes from taking place because of the way in which the administrative bureaucracy was organized. Too many provincial officials had dual loyalties, and when events precipitated revolts or rebellions, their ties were to their neighbors with whom they sided against the central government. If revolutions begin in the more prosperous and less oppressed parts of the state, then the events that immediately precipitated the collapse of Huari political control may have occurred first in the north, where the earliest successor states arose and where there is little evidence of depopulation and economic depression during the last years of the empire.

The Inca Empire

Small regional states with continually changing boundaries and varied political institutions emerged after the fall of the Huari Empire. This pattern persisted into the first half of the fifteenth

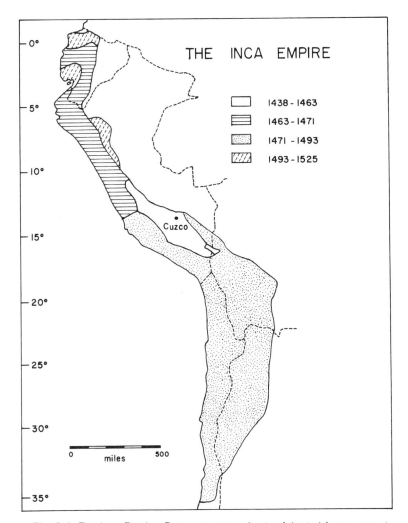

Fig. 5-3. The Inca Empire. Dates are approximate. Adapted from a map by John H. Rowe, "Absolute Chronology in the Andean Area," *American Antiquity* X (no. 3, Menasha, Society for American Archaeology, January 1945) p. 273.

century, until one of them—the Incas from the Cuzco Basin in the south highlands of Peru—rapidly expanded its sphere of influence. By 1525, the Inca Empire stretched from northern Ecuador to central Chile and northwestern Argentina; however, virtually all of the area was conquered during the reigns of two rulers, Pachakuti (1438–1471) and Thupa Inka (1471–1493). The Incas imposed their religion on the conquered groups but allowed them to keep their own religions as long as they served the state one as well. While religion served as the vehicle for their conquests, it is also clear that more important factors were **103** involved. For example, the Incas were able to maintain community self-sufficiency because of their expansion.

Pachakuti rebuilt Cuzco, the political and religious capital of the empire, in order to make it more impressive. At the same time, he also rebuilt the entire Cuzco Basin; rivers were channeled, the valley floor was leveled, and agricultural terraces were built on the surrounding hill slopes. This reclamation project undoubtedly increased the agricultural productivity of the basin. In addition, the emperor—as well as the state and the church—acquired lands throughout the empire. These lands were cultivated by the local communities as a form of tax. Part of the produce from them was used to support the local Inca administrators, while the rest of it was sent to Cuzco where it was used by the Incas for the state and religious officials as well as the emperor, his wives, and their children. These communities also provided the Incas with other goods besides food—for example, textiles or objects made from precious metals.

Inca society—and perhaps Huari society as well—had two peculiar features. First, no ruler could inherit anything from his predecessor. The property of a dead ruler passed to his other descendants who formed a royal corporation and supported themselves from his lands and the labor taxes owed him. Consequently, a new emperor had to acquire land and labor to support his corporation and government. This placed a continually increasing burden on the provincial communities as they were required to provide land and services for four rulers between 1438 and 1532. It must have been particularly burdensome after 1493, when the empire virtually stopped expanding.

The second feature was that there was no recognized order of succession to the throne. Consequently, much tension accompanied determination of succession, and rival groups put forth their own candidates. Each emperor dealt with this problem in his own way. Pachakuti stepped down and named his most capable son as ruler. Thupa Inka married his sister and named their young son as his successor. For several years, regents governed the empire until Wayna Qhapaq was old enough to assume the responsibilities for himself. When he died unexpectedly around 1527 without designating his successor, the empire was almost immediately thrown into chaos as rival groups fought for the throne. During the ensuing civil war, the power of the empire was substantially diminished, as one community sided with one faction, a second community sided with another group, and a third community tried to remain independent or break away from the empire altogether. The Spaniards arrived in 1532 in the midst of this conflict and, for several years, were regarded by many Andean peoples as just another faction in the dispute.

The Spaniards ultimately played an important role in the

collapse of the Inca Empire; however, the seeds of its destruction were already deeply imbedded in the organization of the state. The Incas allowed the conquered communities to maintain their identities and regional affiliations; they placed increasingly oppressive burdens on their subjects, particularly after the empire stopped growing; and they were unable to regain the power and authority that was lost during the war over succession.

STATE FORMATION IN MESOAMERICA

The peoples of Mesoamerica organized themselves very differently from those of the central Andes. The members of an Andean group attempted to control all of the resources they needed. Goods immediately available to one part of the group were exchanged for goods immediately available to other parts of the same group living in environments with different resources. Exchange took place primarily between members of the same group because of the ideal of self-sufficiency and the distribution of resources in the area.

The Mesoamerican Pattern: Market Exchange

In Mesoamerica, an ethnic group controlled only those resources that were available locally and exchanged them with other groups for commodities that its members could not provide for themselves. Exchange was primarily between groups living in different areas rather than between members of the same group. Each group depended on a number of other units and participated with them in a large-scale exchange network. This pattern of interdependence led to the development and elaboration of a market economy—an institution that was virtually unknown in the Andean area before the arrival of the Europeans.

Mesoamerica is an environmentally diverse area characterized by ecological extremes from tropical rain forest to scrub desert. The patterning of its diversity is very different from that in the central Andes, largely because of different relative positions with respect to major zones of atmospheric circulation. It is difficult to describe the differences of patterning in a few words; however, it is perhaps useful to visualize both areas as large grids of multicolored squares, in which each color represents a different environmental zone. There would be repetitive sequences of color on the Andean grid; it would resemble a complex, but fairly regular checkerboard. These repetitive sequences of color would largely be absent on the Mesoamerican grid; instead of a checkerboard, it would resemble a complex mosaic made by an artist who deliberately attempted to randomize the color of each square.

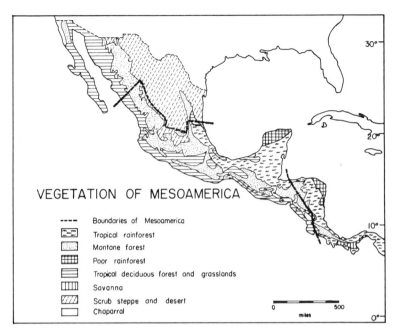

Fig. 5–4. Vegetation of Mesoamerica.

This difference has important implications concerning the distribution of resources and where people had to go to acquire them. The linear and repetitive arrangements of resource areas, described earlier for the Andes, would also exist in Mesoamerica, and the resources could be exploited as they were in the Andes. Ethnic groups living in similar settings in adjacent areas would have access to roughly the same set of resources. However, what would happen to a Mesoamerican group that lived near the boundary between major environmental zones rather than in the middle of one? This situation occurred much more frequently in Mesoamerica than it did in the Andes. Its members might produce one set of goods while their neighbors might produce entirely different ones because of environmental differences. Since they viewed many of these "foreign" commodities as desirable or even necessary for life, the members of a typical Mesoamerican community had to rely on other groups to provide them, because they could not produce these goods themselves.

Commercial networks were well developed in Mesoamerica by 1500 B.C. Unfortunately, we know very little about the origins and early stages of development of these networks, because there is a relative void in the archaeological data for the period from roughly 3000 to 1500 B.C., when many of these developments presumably took place. Perhaps these commercial networks originated with the spread of cultivated plants from regions where they occurred naturally to regions where they did not or could not be grown successfully after they were introduced. If so, then the economic interdependency of groups was an ancient cultural pattern in Mesoamerica.

This commerce took place in a highly diversified social and economic setting. Some groups had large populations with considerable status differentiation and craft specialization. Others were smaller, less differentiated socially, and supported fewer or different craft specialities. Some groups produced large amounts of food, because the agricultural potential of their territories was high or because they were able to assimilate new agricultural techniques or crops with the passage of time. Others lacked such advantages. Regional variation of this sort was already very apparent in Mesoamerica by 1500 B.C. and was superimposed on the equally diverse environmental setting of the area. Well-endowed regions—such as the Valley of Mexico, Oaxaca, and the Mixteca Alta—were always important in Mesoamerican history, while their less well-endowed neighbors—the Gulf Coast, the Yucatán Peninsula, or the far southern periphery of the area—were never influential or were important for only brief intervals of time.

The Olmec

The first burst of extensive, long-distance exchange began about 1100 B.C. and was associated with the spread of Olmec influence apparently from the Gulf Coast lowlands of southern Vera Cruz and Tabasco to other parts of Mesoamerica. As early as 1400 B.C., the inhabitants of San Lorenzo Tenochtitlán, a site in Vera Cruz that later became a major Olmec center, were importing obsidian from a number of sources—including Teotihuacán, Pachuca, and El Chayal in the eastern highlands of Guatemala. These localities are two to three hundred miles from San Lorenzo. By 1100 B.C., the Gulf Coast groups were importing other foreign materials as well: basalt, jade, serpentine, magnetite, and hematite to name only a few of the nonperishable goods that have been found in Olmec sites on the Gulf Coast and do not occur naturally in the area. The quantities of exotic raw materials imported by Olmec communities on the Gulf Coast were truly impressive, when we consider that nearly 5000 tons of imported serpentine have been found at a single Olmec center —La Venta which is located in Tabasco. The volume of this commerce becomes even more impressive in light of the fact that land transport in Mesoamerica was always largely dependent on foot porters.

During the period when the Gulf Coast Olmec groups were importing these goods, the area had probably the largest nucleated settlements in all of Mesoamerica. These large settlements with all of their public architecture provided a favorable social environment for the development of craft specialization and considerable differences of status and wealth among their inhabitants. Food supplies were probably fairly secure in the area from one year to the next and were based on agricultural production supplemented by game and aquatic resources from nearby streams and lagoons. Clearly, the Gulf Coast Olmec groups could sustain themselves on the resources that were available locally. Equally clear, however, was the fact that they wanted and imported commodities or materials controlled by groups living elsewhere in Mesoamerica.

The Olmec people entered into exchange relationships with stratified groups, which were probably only slightly less socially differentiated than themselves. These groups, mostly in the highlands, lived in large nucleated settlements in areas with high agricultural and demographic potentials—Oaxaca, Puebla, Morelos, or the Valley of Mexico. Each area contained some exotic raw material that the Olmec people wanted. Around Oaxaca, for example, the material was magnetite, which was used for making small mirrors. At the present time, we can distinguish two major patterns in these exchange relationships. First, there were small colonies of Gulf Coast Olmec peoples living at a few strategic localities in central Mexico—particularly in Morelos and Puebla and perhaps in Guerrero as well. They controlled the flow of goods through their settlements. Olmec goods entered the highlands through these settlements, and any highland products leaving the area were shipped to the coast from them. Second, the elite groups in other areas—most notably Oaxaca—had direct commercial ties with the Gulf Coast Olmec settlements. These relationships were reciprocal in the sense that both the Gulf Coast Olmec communities and the highland elite groups benefited from them; however, since this commerce was imbedded in the social matrix of the times, these benefits were not necessarily obvious economic ones. For example, the elite group of the Valley of Oaxaca, who were already distinguishing themselves from the rest of their society by wearing ornaments made from imported exotic materials, apparently controlled the flow of magnetite to the Gulf Coast Olmec communities. In return, they were apparently the ones who acquired some of the behavior, status symbols, religious ideas and practices, and perhaps even the language of the Olmec elite groups. These acquisitions enhanced their prestige within their own communities and served to differentiate them even more from the rest of the local population.

The elite groups of the Gulf Coast Olmec settlements may well have used the materials they imported to enhance their local prestige and to maintain the status differential they enjoyed in their own communities. The buried serpentine pavements at La Venta, which were obviously not meant to be seen by anyone, suggest that the Olmec elite group in this community deliberately kept the supply of this material scarce, so that individuals with lower status in their community could not afford to acquire significant quantities of it. In a sense, they "killed" the serpentine in the pavements by taking a valuable, but indestructible, commodity out of circulation rather than stockpiling it. By doing so, they maintained the value of this good as both scarce and foreign. By continuing to maintain social and commercial relations with the suppliers of serpentine, the elite group also ensured that a steady supply of it would arrive at La Venta and that its members could maintain their status differential, because they controlled its availability and abundance in the community.

The exotic raw materials imported by the Olmec elite changed through time. Magnetite, hematite, and ilmenite were some of the more important ones at first. After about 900 B.C., jade seems to have become increasingly important, while the importance of the earlier imports either remained constant or even diminished. These changes may reflect nothing more than shifts in taste; however, they may also reflect attempts by the Olmec elite groups to maintain, reaffirm, or even reestablish their status differentials within their own communities after a particular exotic material had become too common. Whatever the reasons underlying these changes, their effect was that the Olmec elite groups emphasized social and economic relations with a continually changing series of highland elite groups who had access to different desirable materials. Consequently, exchange relationships with a highland area that were particularly important for the Olmec elite groups at 1000 B.C. may have been unimportant or even nonexistent five hundred years later.

As their ties with the Gulf Coast Olmec communities gradually withered away, highland elite groups also modified their exchange relationships to fit new patterns of prestige that were appearing within the highlands. Formerly unimportant communities gradually acquired prestige as their production and population increased. The highland elite groups established ties with other communities and entered new commercial networks that would presumably allow them to maintain the status differentials in their own communities and would continue to stimulate local economic growth. As a result, the exchange network dominated by the Gulf Coast Olmec communities was gradually replaced by a series of regional networks dominated by various highland ethnic groups, once they caught up with and eventually surpassed the Olmecs in terms of prestige.

The post-Olmec exchange networks appeared at various times;

for example, one centered at Tlatilco in the Valley of Mexico may have emerged as early as 800 B.C., while another centered at Monte Alban in the Valley of Oaxaca appeared about 500 B.C. None of them was as large as the one that the Olmec communities had dominated earlier. There was probably a great deal of continuity between the Olmec and post-Olmec exchange networks, involving the same routes and many of the same commodities; however, the volume of exchange may have been smaller, and the goods may have been moved over shorter distances.

Teotihuacán

An exchange network dominated by the inhabitants of Teotihuacán emerged about 2000 years ago in central Mexico, and by A.D. 350 it was the largest and most important one in Mesoamerica. As you will recall from the last chapter, this was the period of rapid economic and demographic growth at Teotihuacán. Other factors—besides the obsidian, its agricultural productivity, and its participation simultaneously in several exchange networks— probably favored the growth of Teotihuacán at the expense of other communities in central Mexico. It was located at the crossroads of several major trade routes that led to other highland regions and to the Gulf Coast, and it was an important holy place or ceremonial center that was visited by pilgrims from all over Mesoamerica who undoubtedly did more than pray and make offerings to the gods while they were in the city.

Teotihuacán influence was much more pervasive and extensive in Mesoamerica than Olmec influence had been earlier. Let us consider just the kinds of nonperishable goods that were moved around by the two groups. The Olmec group exported mainly luxury goods—small jade figurines and an occasional sculpture. The *teotihuacanos* exported both luxury products and utilitarian goods—like obsidian tools and ordinary pottery—that must have been used by the commoners as well as the elite members of the recipient groups. Teotihuacán objects, even the utilitarian ones, have a far wider geographical distribution than the Olmec luxury goods.

Teotihuacán influence is very apparent in some regions and virtually absent in others, suggesting that the ethnic groups incorporated into the exchange system it dominated did not have to be contiguous with each other. Instead, other factors apparently played more important roles in determining the *teotihuacanos'* decisions with whom to trade and by what form of exchanges. What did the other group have or control? Was it really worthwhile to have or control access to this commodity? How far away was the community and how big was its population? Would they

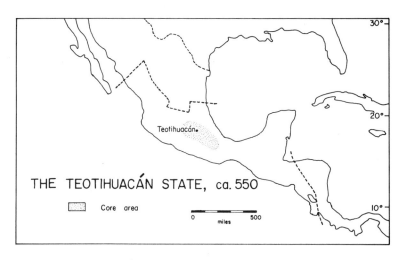

Fig. 5–5. The Teotihuacán State, ca. A.D. 550.

fight if attacked openly? Was there another way to get what they had? As a result of such variables, Teotihuacán influence, like Olmec influence before it, took various forms: they traded, collected tribute, colonized, or conquered. At the same time, other communities were also deciding how they should deal with the people of Teotihuacán. Some of them changed their identities and, in effect, became cultural *teotihuacanos,* while others steadfastly maintained their own identities and even their independence.

The best evidence for Teotihuacán conquest and colonization comes from Guatemala. The *teotihuacanos* apparently conquered Kaminaljuyu, a highland site on the outskirts of Guatemala City, and erected a large building complex in their own architectural style at the center of the site. In addition, Teotihuacán goods have been found in a number of elite burials. They established a colony of sorts at Tikal, a Maya site in the eastern lowlands, where there is a small building complex in Teotihuacán style and the representation of a Teotihuacán warrior on one of the stelae. Clearly, there were resident Teotihuacán populations at both settlements.

The *teotihuacanos* had strong economic incentives for conquering Kaminaljuyu and establishing a colony there, because it was probably the major distribution center in southern Mesoamerica for three important commodities—obsidian, cacao, and jade. By conquering it, they not only gained some control over the flow of these goods but also acquired a ready-made market for the goods they were producing in the workshops at home. The control they acquired over the flow of obsidian and cacao was particularly important. By dealing in obsidian from the nearby deposit at El Chayal, Kaminaljuyu was in direct competition with

111

Teotihuacán for control of the Mesoamerican obsidian market. Once the *teotihuacanos* gained access to the El Chayal obsidian, they had a virtual monopoly on the obsidian supply and trade, since they already controlled the two other major sources during this period—their own and the one at Pachuca. Cacao, which was highly valued by the Aztecs, was already important enough at this time to be represented in murals at Teotihuacán. For several centuries before they conquered Kaminaljuyu, the *teotihuacanos* had been in close contact with the Tajín communities of the Gulf Coast that, in later times at least, were among the important suppliers of cacao in Mesoamerica. They probably got most of their cacao from these groups during this period; however, Kaminaljuyu was the distribution center for the second largest cacao-producing area in Mesoamerica and, once the *teotihuacanos* conquered it, they gained access to much more cacao than they had earlier and must have played a much more prominent role in its distribution. Their motives for establishing a colony in Tikal were also economic ones. They acquired new markets for their goods and greater supplies of products from the Maya lowlands—copal, feathers, and perhaps slaves.

As Teotihuacán influence became confined to the Valley of Mexico and then to the Teotihuacán Valley itself between A.D. 650 and 800, the small, regional exchange networks became much more important in other parts of Mesoamerica. The fortunes of these networks changed through time, as one group and then another gained control of them. Various groups competed to fill the power vacuum created by the collapse of Teotihuacán. This period of fragmentation and political chaos reigned for nearly 350 years. It was a time when warfare seems to have been a common feature of everyday life. Fortified settlements were built, warrior figures were represented on stelae in the Maya area, and the Bonampak murals depict raids and captive taking.

The Toltecs and Aztecs

The Toltecs of central Mexico acquired some degree of political and economic dominance in northern Mesoamerica between A.D. 850 and 1200, even though their influence was not as extensive as that of their predecessors from Teotihuacán. The capital of the Toltec state was Tula, located in the Teotlalpan region north of the Valley of Mexico on the periphery of the old Teotihuacán Empire. Economically, the Teotlalpan was and is an unstable area because of its position on the margins of two major environmental zones. When the rains are good, agriculture can be practiced in the area; however, when the rainfall belt shifts slightly southward, agricultural production becomes difficult in these marginal farmlands. At the time Tula was founded—nearly a thousand years ago according to historical annals that cannot be dated very accurately or around A.D. 500 according to some recent radiocarbon dates—farming peoples occupied the Teotlalpan. However, rainfall diminished in the area after about A.D. 1250, and, when the Spaniards arrived some three centuries later, it was inhabited by nomadic bands of hunters and gatherers.

The Toltecs looked northward to prevent incursions by nomadic groups who would upset the delicate ecological balance that existed in their territory. They established frontier garrisons at places like La Quemada in order to prevent the *chichimeca,* or wandering peoples, from overrunning them or to incorporate these groups as auxiliary but integral parts of their society. Some of the frontier *chichimeca* probably became farmers and served as mercenaries in the Toltec armies. The Toltecs looked in other directions in order to acquire the goods they could not produce locally. Like their predecessors from Teotihuacán, they expanded largely into the rich lands to the south and east where cacao, jade, and feathers were found. They traded, collected tribute, and conquered peoples in order to get what they needed. What these communities received from the Toltecs in exchange for their goods may ultimately boil down to nothing more than obsidian or an obsidian dagger in the heart. The full extent of the Toltec state is not known with certainty at this time. It undoubtedly included the area from Michoacán to northern Vera Cruz and the northern part of the Valley of Mexico.

The historical annals of the Toltecs indicate that power in Tula was divided between sacred and secular rulers. When one of the sacred rulers tried illegally to pass his office to a member of his own family, a civil war ensued, and he and his followers were driven from the city. The internal strife accompanying this dispute seriously undermined the power of the state and, ultimately, was one of the factors involved in its disintegration. As the state began to fall apart, various groups seized control of different areas and established new successor states that were little more than smaller versions of the Toltec Empire itself. These groups, whether or not they were actual descendants of the Toltecs, called themselves Toltecs in order to justify their claims to the lands, peoples, and tribute of the old empire. There were several of these successor states in the Valley of Mexico alone, and similar political formations emerged in other parts of Mesoamerica as well—for example, at Chichen Itza in the Yucatán Peninsula, Cholula, and in highland Guatemala. *Chichimeca* groups also moved into the area from the north, and some of them eventually established their own domains. This only compounded the confusion that already surrounded the collapse of Tula's power.

One group, called the Mexica at first and then the Aztecs,

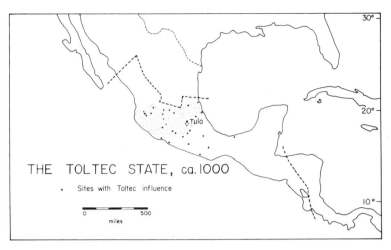

Fig. 5–6. The Toltec State, ca. A.D. 1000.

settled in the Valley of Mexico about A.D. 1200. Three centuries later, they dominated much of Mesoamerica through trade and conquest. When the Aztecs first arrived in the valley, they were little more than the clients of more powerful groups who gave them land in return for military service. The Aztecs were a very quarrelsome group who found it exceedingly difficult to get along with the peoples they served or their allies. At first, they served in the armies of Atzcapotzalco, which was the most powerful group in the Valley of Mexico at that time. However, as a result of internal strife over succession to the throne, the Aztecs lost their favored position in this state about 1427. They rebelled against their lords and allied themselves with the Acolhua who lived on the island of Texcoco on the western side of the lake. Together, they defeated the peoples of Atzcapotzalco three years later. In 1430, the Aztec and Acolhua entered into an alliance with another group called the Tlacopan, and the three of them divided the Valley of Mexico and most of Mesoamerica into separate spheres of influence.

During the next seventy years, the Aztecs brought most of the peoples of central Mexico under the rule of the "Triple Alliance" and raided or conquered all the way to the Guatemalan border. By 1515, they were the dominant power in this alliance, because they imposed puppet rulers on the thrones of the other two and concentrated their tribute payments in the Aztec treasury. They received enormous sums of annual tribute payments from their subjects. For example, they received at least 100,000 cotton cloaks each year and perhaps as many as 2 million since there is a factor of about twenty in the tribute counts that can be interpreted in different ways. Part of this tribute, whatever its size, was redistributed among the warrior groups, but the bulk of it was used to purchase luxury goods for the nobility and the king. These luxury items were probably acquired largely by the *pochtecas*, a semiautonomous class in the Aztec state, that specialized in trading high-value commodities over long distances. The state protected their trade routes and avenged attacks on them. In return, the merchants spied on their customers and provided the state with information about them.

The Mesoamerican pattern of empire building was very different from the Andean one. The Mesoamerican groups often preferred raids to permanent occupation and collecting tribute to establishing some form of permanent political control. Their states rarely consisted of continuous expanses of land; instead, there were large areas within the empire that maintained their independence, because their inhabitants were too powerful to be subjugated or because they had nothing that the expanding community wanted. Like the Andean peoples, the Mesoamerican empire builders established strong, cohesive imperial structures but the subject groups retained much of their own identities and hatred for the conquerors. The Spaniards recognized this fact in both areas and quickly exploited it to their own advantage.

THE RISE AND FALL OF STATES

In the preceding sections, we saw that the Andean and Mesoamerican states were based on different principles of acquiring scarce resources. The Andean states attempted to control directly all of the resources they needed, while the Mesoamerican ones ensured that other groups provided the goods and services they

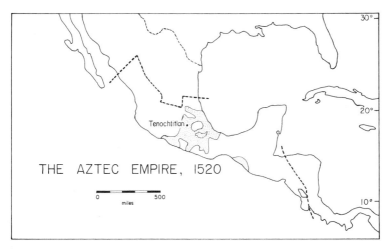

Fig. 5–7. The Aztec Empire, A.D. 1520.

could not provide for themselves. The states that appeared in other areas—for example, Colombia—may have been organized on the basis of principles that were different from either of these.

One mechanism that may have triggered off the process of state formation in the Andes and Mesoamerica was population pressure on resources. Population pressure comprises several factors: the demand for resources created by the population of a given area, the definition of resources, the kinds of technology used to exploit them, and their supply in the community's territory. When a particular resource is so abundant that the members of a community have access to as much as they want of it, there is no pressure on that resource. However, when their demand for the resource surpasses its availability, population pressure begins to appear.

In both the Andes and Mesoamerica, communities were competing for access to scarce resources rather than abundant ones. The successful groups became preeminent as their members gained control of the means of producing or acquiring more of the scarce commodities. The less successful communities were occasionally driven from their lands, but, more frequently, they were hemmed in because there was no place for them to go. Even if other resources were available, as often as not neighboring groups already controlled access to these products. One alternative was to subordinate themselves in some way to the dominant group—to pay a price for their continued existence, whether this involved trying to raise production, lowering their standard of living, paying tribute, or even losing their autonomy.

The dominant group was the innovative force in the formation of the state in the sense that its members experimented with new ideas and perhaps techniques as well for acquiring greater supplies of the scarce resources they needed. From their viewpoint, the standard of living improved after the state was formed, because they were consuming or using greater quantities of the scarce items. At first, only the elite groups of the community may have experienced the benefits of this increased consumption; however, as time passed they gradually filtered down to larger segments of the population, at varying degrees and rates.

Increased consumption can generate new opportunities and stimulate production, as the population creates new needs once the old ones are satisfied. This very process of economic growth can also set up tensions within the state, as new demands and burdens are placed on its subjects. These can range from increased taxes or tribute to support the existing institutions of the state to demands for greater and greater proportions of the scarce resources. When the demands surpass the productive capacity of the state, segments of the population begin to resist the very changes that are needed for its continued growth. It becomes increasingly difficult for people—particularly those with vested interests or ties to outmoded institutions—to conceive of new ways of living or of new ways of doing things. When these changes do not occur, the difficulties grow and conditions become progressively worse.

States decline as they lose their preeminence. In some instances, they are surpassed by faster-growing states, whose communities are more willing to experiment with new ideas and ways for acquiring what they want. The decline is a relative one, since both states may be growing. One is growing faster than the other, however. In other instances, states decline because of the internal problems they generate. They disintegrate, because the tensions and alienation that exist are neglected. Sectors of the population that can bring about the changes required for continued growth are unwilling to institute them, while those that want to carry out the changes are usually unable to do so.

6. Ecology, Economy, and Population

The themes emphasized throughout this book are all tied either to the complex interactions between human groups and their social and natural environments, or to the variations in these relationships in both time and space. Let us now examine some implications of these themes in more detail.

THE ENVIRONMENT AND RESOURCES

In most situations, hundreds of different species of plants and animals live in close proximity to each other. Human populations depend on the activities of many other species and interact with them. They acquire energy from some of these organisms by using them for food and fuel, and compete with others for energy, when they utilize the same plants or animals that are consumed by these organisms. And, they change the physical environments of many species when they cut down trees, put fertilizer on the ground, or build houses.

Species are usually not uniformly distributed throughout a given area, but tend to cluster where the prevailing conditions favor their continued existence. Each species has a range of physical conditions that it can tolerate in the sense that its members can live and reproduce successfully when they exist but cannot otherwise. Generally, these tolerance ranges are relatively small for plants and insects and relatively large for most mammals. The distribution of each species is also affected by other species that compete or interfere with its members in some way.

Human populations are rarely concerned with the distribution of every species, because they always rely on a very small portion of the total number that resides in close proximity to them. These are the ones that provide them with energy or the ones that they try to eliminate as competitors or pests. They generally ignore the distributions of other species, and even their existence, even though these organisms may occupy vital positions in human food chains. Since most human populations also have food preferences, taboos, and differential success at exploiting the various species around them, they do not use all of the potential food resources uniformly. For example, some edible species may not be consumed at all, while others may be overexploited to the point of local extinction.

Human populations define the carrying capacity of the areas where they live by deciding which of the species that live around them constitute food and how much of these various foods they need to sustain themselves. Because of their food preferences and strategies for resource acquisition, the members of a particular group may completely exhaust the available supplies of some resources and use only small portions of the available supplies of others.

By virtue of their behavior patterns and position as plant and animal "predators" in food chains, human populations are incredibly inefficient users of the total amounts of energy that are available to them. For example, it appears that the fifteenth-century inhabitants of the Hay Hollow Valley in eastern Arizona never utilized more than 5 percent of the total biomass of the area. This means that they were acquiring an infinitesimally small portion—a fraction of 1 percent—of the total amount of energy available in the valley. Estimates of energy consumption on this order of magnitude are probably appropriate for most other populations in the New World as well.

Because of this inefficiency, human populations are particularly susceptible to changes in the amounts of energy that are available to them, whether the changes were brought about by the actions of the group itself or by changes of temperature, wind conditions, or the availability of effective moisture. Groups that exploit a broad spectrum of resources have a better chance of maintaining themselves in the face of changing environmental conditions than those that exploit only limited ranges of resources.

Changes in the physical conditions that prevail in an area can have both long-term and short-term effects on the biotic environment and on the availability and abundance of different food resources. Long-term environmental changes occur most often in areas near the margins of major meteorological zones. Northwest Peru is one of these areas. It is the climatically unstable area between the zone of heavy tropical rainfall of northern Ecuador and the intensely arid zone of coastal Peru to the south. In late glacial and early postglacial times, the Ecuadorian rainfall belt was displaced southward from its present position, and northwest Peru received enough annual rainfall to support mangrove swamp communities in the estuary systems along the coast. At 6000 B.C., the inhabitants of the area were still relying extensively on two species of molluscs that live exclusively in mangrove swamps. These species composed nearly 100 percent of the shellfish consumed throughout the year. However, when the tropical rainfall belt retreated northward toward its present position, northwest Peru no longer received enough rainfall to support the mangrove vegetation and its associated fauna. In response to this change in their biotic environment, the inhabitants were forced to move their settlements to other localities in the area and to begin exploiting new kinds of marine resources. Not a single mangrove mollusc has been found in any archaeological site in the area that dates to the last five or six thousand years.

Short-term fluctuations in the weather constitute a random or fortuitous factor in the relationship between the biotic environment and the availability and abundance of food resources. The effects can be either beneficial or deleterious to the population, depending on what happened. For example, a few years ago, summer temperatures on the north coast of Peru were about 2 to 3° F. warmer than they normally are at the present time. It so happens that the particular variety of rice cultivated in this area is much more productive when the summer temperatures are slightly warmer than usual. The increased temperatures of that summer permitted the rice plants to germinate earlier and grow longer. Rice harvests increased by roughly 50 percent from the normal 8000 kilograms a year to a little more than 12,000 kilograms. One obvious consequence of this exceptionally good harvest was that much more rice was available to the population that consumes this crop. Alternatively, a reduction in the temperature or the amount of effective moisture may result in exceptionally low harvests or occasionally in none at all.

A glance at agricultural statistics—such as those published by the Department of Agriculture—shows that harvest sizes are rarely constant from one year to the next. Instead, they vary, often significantly, around some average size. A year with an exceptionally good harvest may be followed by two or three years with average harvests, and these may be followed by a year or two with lower than average harvests. The point is that the total amount of food available to a population is rarely constant from one year to the next. In situations where a population is approaching its maximum size or has already arrived at this level given its economic orientation, these fluctuations in the amount of food available can have significant consequences.

RESOURCES AND POPULATION

The size of a technologically stationary population is ultimately set by its food supply. The population grows until it reaches the maximum level allowed by its environment and the use that its members make of the resources available to them. As we have already seen, this level, or carrying capacity, can vary considerably from one stationary population to another, even if they were occupying exactly the same area and exploiting the same general environment. The two groups might have different standards of living, or they might perceive different elements of their environment as usable resources and have different strategies for acquiring them.

When a population moves into a previously unoccupied area or adopts some innovation that increases its food supply, its numbers increase rapidly at first. However, as the population size approaches the carrying capacity of the environment, its growth rate begins to diminish. Occasionally, technologically stationary populations, which are closed in the sense that neither immigration nor emigration occur, may overshoot this level and temporarily deplete all of the available food supplies. Their numbers then decrease to a level below that of the carrying capacity and eventually increase again as food becomes at least temporarily more abundant. In this pattern, population numbers oscillate with a continually decreasing amplitude around the carrying capacity of the environment and eventually stabilize themselves with respect to this level.

There are both short-term and long-term changes in the sizes of nonindustrial populations. Recent surveys of the demography of nonindustrial populations—both in Europe before the Industrial Revolution and elsewhere—contain some interesting information concerning these changes, that are probably applicable in a

Fig. 6–1. *a*, The standard of living is plotted as a function of population. The optimum population, N_o, occurs where the individual standard of living is greatest. The individual standard of living increases as the population approaches this level and decreases once this level is surpassed. *b*, The standard of living and total production are plotted as functions of population. *c*, Standard of living, total production, and marginal productivity are plotted as functions of population. Notice that the maximum marginal productivity MP_o is reached well before the population attains its optimum size N_o or where the total production P_o begins to diminish with the addition of another individual to the population. Figures 12, 13 and 14 from pages 43 and 44 in *General Theory of Population* by Alfred Sauvy. © 1969 by George Weidenfeld and Nicolson, Ltd., London. Originally published under the title *Theorie Generale de la Population;* © 1966 by Presses Universitaires de France. Basic Books Publishers, Inc., New York, and George Weidenfeld and Nicolson, Ltd., London.

PRODUCTION AND POPULATION

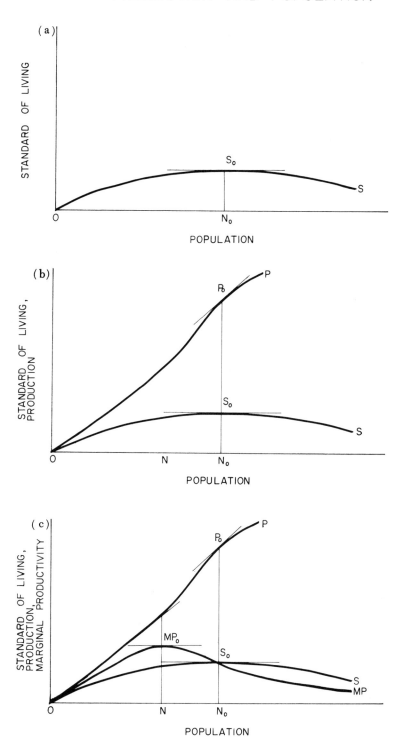

general sense to what happened in the New World. For purposes of analyzing short-term fluctuations, let us assume for the moment that we are dealing with a closed, technologically stationary population. In such a situation, the population can grow only when the number of births exceeds the number of deaths each year, and decrease only if deaths exceed births.

Birth rates rarely exceed 45 to 50 individuals per 1000 each year in nonindustrial populations, except when they have very unusual age structures in which there is a greater than normally expected number of mating adults. Birth rates are rarely less than 15 individuals per 1000 each year. This means that the maximum rate of potential population growth varies within a relatively narrow range—from about 1.5 to 5 percent a year. However, no population grows at anywhere near its maximum potential rate, because deaths do occur. In nonindustrial populations, death rates vary over a much wider range than birth rates. In good years, they may be slightly lower than the birth rates or roughly equal to them. In bad years, they may be as high as 200 to 400 individuals per 1000. It is clear that the size of a population would diminish considerably if there were several bad years in a row and death rates on this order of magnitude prevailed. Bad years, in the demographic sense, are often very regional in their occurrence because of local harvest failures or the spread of an epidemic that affects only a small area.

The ultimate causes of high death rates in an area are most often epidemics, famines resulting from poor harvests, and events like wars in which crops are destroyed, diseases are introduced, and men are taken from their lands. During periods of high mortality in Europe, at least, death was rarely due to starvation but rather to diseases and infections that were induced and aggravated by inadequate food supplies. It is also clear that periods of high mortality in an area do not always indicate that it was overpopulated; however, the proportion of a population that dies during a bad year is probably somewhat higher when its numbers are approaching the carrying capacity of their environment.

High death rates tend to weed out the most vulnerable members of a population. This weeding-out period is often followed by an interval of relatively low death rates among the survivors and of relatively high birth rates. The increase in the number of births means that a generation later—roughly fifteen to twenty years—there is a relatively sudden increase in the number of individuals reaching mating age. As they conceive, there is another relatively sudden increase in births, and as their offspring come of age and mate, there is still another increase, although this one tends to be less sudden and obvious. What has happened is that the high death rates of the bad years have set up a "wave effect" in the population curve that has a periodicity of about one generation and a continually decreasing amplitude. This wave effect is obscured by factors such as the kinds of marriage patterns that exist in the population or the occurrence of another set of bad years.

Short-term fluctuations in the New World are affected by other variables. Demographic crises occur more frequently in some areas and periods than in others. Populations with relatively undiversified economies, for example, apparently suffer bad years more often and more acutely than those with highly diversified economic orientations. The impact of bad years seems to be less extreme, at least in terms of death rates, among large local populations than among small ones. Immigration and emigration have certainly played much more important roles than we have attributed to them. We have to assess the importance of these and other variables in order to gain a clearer understanding of the kinds of short-term population fluctuations that have occurred in the New World.

The basic long-term change was one of growth. The total population of the Americas has increased substantially from the time the first immigrants arrived about 25,000 years ago to the time when Europeans and African slaves began to arrive in significant numbers during the early sixteenth century. The amount of this growth, as well as the rate at which it occurred, depends largely on the estimates accepted of the native American population on the eve of the European conquest. These range from about 3,000,000 persons to more than 100,000,000 persons for the entire New World, with recent research favoring a figure much closer to the larger estimate.

There were at least two obvious factors involved in the long-term trend and probably many more obscure ones. For instance, populations moved into previously uninhabited environments where plant and animal foods were relatively more abundant than they had been in the areas where the groups lived earlier. Or, there were innovations—both technological and organizational—that permitted these populations to exploit their environments more fully or to alter them in such ways that food became more plentiful. In both situations, the nutritional levels of the populations increased, which eventually led to an increase in their sizes.

The long-term fluctuations in this upward trend are even more difficult to account for. Some have suggested that the stable or declining portions of population growth curves are the result of changes in the physical environment which lowered the carrying capacity of certain areas. Others have suggested that epidemic diseases raised death rates over broad areas or for considerable spans of time. These are complex situations, and we undoubtedly will not understand them by referring to single-factor explanations; however, each explanation may play some role in developing a fuller understanding of what actually happened.

POPULATION AND ECONOMY

At any moment in time, the size of a population is determined by a complex set of factors including its birth and death rates, its perception of what constitutes resources, and its ability to acquire and distribute these resources to its members. A change in any one of these factors may ultimately lead to changes in the other factors, as well as in the size of the population itself. For instance, an innovation that significantly reduces the death rate of a community over a fairly long period of time—such as the adoption of antibiotic medicines—would eventually lead to an increase in the size of its population; however, if this were not accompanied by another innovation that raised the production and consumption of energy by the members of the group and if they were already living close to the carrying capacity of their environment when the mortality-reducing innovation was adopted, then the increase in population would ultimately lower the average standard of living, as each individual acquired progressively less of the fixed amount of energy that was available.

Suppose a community adopts an innovation that allows its members to produce and consume a little more energy than they did previously and, at the same time, that their birth and death rates remain unchanged. Assuming for the moment that everyone in the community uses roughly the same amount of the available energy, the adoption of this innovation can affect either the size of the population, its standard of living, or both. Probably most typical when a community produces and consumes more energy is when both its population and standard of living are increasing at the same time. If the population growth rate of the community lags a little behind its economic growth rate, then its members will experience an increase in their standard of living. The duration of this improved living standard may be temporary or relatively long lasting, depending on the nature of the innovation. If the innovation allows the community to produce only a little more energy than the amount that was already available, then the improved living standard will be a temporary one; however, if the innovation has the potential for opening up large amounts of previously untapped energy—as the introduction of irrigation agriculture seems to have done on the central coast of Peru—then an ever higher standard of living may become an almost permanent feature of the economy, as long as population growth continues to lag behind economic growth.

For the moment, suppose everyone in a community produces

and consumes the same amount of energy. When its population is too small the community is unable to use all of the energy potentially available, and the standard of living is lower than it could be. When the population is too large, even if the community uses all of the available energy, its standard of living is low because each person gets such a small share. Somewhere between these two extremes, there is an optimum population size for energy production and consumption enabling each individual to use a maximum amount of the energy available, given the economic orientation of his community. The community's standard of living increases as its population size approaches this optimum level, and it decreases once the size of its population exceeds this optimum.

This is due to changes in the marginal productivity of the community—or the increase in the amount of the potentially available energy that occurs when one productive individual is added to the population. When the size of the population is well below its optimum level, each member is producing and consuming only a fraction of the total amount of energy that is potentially available, and his standard of living is lower than it would be if all of the available resources were being used more efficiently. The addition of a productive individual to the population means that the community as a whole is producing and consuming a little more energy than it did previously and that its standard of living increased slightly as a result of this addition. The addition of a second productive individual means that the community is using still more of the potentially available energy and that its standard of living has increased even further. Eventually, however, population growth will reach a point—still well below its optimum size—where the addition of another producer to the community will begin to reduce the rate at which the standard of living is increasing. The living standard will continue to rise for a while, however, though at a continually decreasing rate as the population approaches its optimum size. Once this level is reached, the addition of one more person to the community will actually begin to reduce the average standard of living.

Various factors besides resources affect the optimum population size of a community. Some of these are the proportion of producers to nonproducers in the community, inequalities in the distribution of energy—goods and services—to its members, and the kinds of technological and organizational innovations they decide to adopt.

Virtually every community is composed of both producers and nonproducers—individuals that add or do not add to the energy produced and consumed by the group as a whole. The most obvious examples of nonproducers in many communities are the very young and the very old. Nonproducers have two important effects on the community. First, they reduce the community's standard of living and its maximum population size from what it would be if everyone in the group were a producer. The extent of these reductions depends not only on the proportion of non-producers but also on their patterns of consumption. Second, they increase the optimum population size of the community.

Inequalities in the distribution and consumption of energy mean that some individuals in a community have higher standards of living than others. This characteristic of many societies in the New World affected their population structures. First, these inequalities lower the maximum possible population size of a community. Imagine a group living at the carrying capacity of its environment and at the absolute minimum level necessary to sustain life, in which everyone utilizes exactly the same amount of energy. Then consider what happens when some individuals in the group begin to consume more energy, and the total amount of energy available to the population does not change. Those individuals who give up energy are eventually eliminated from the population, because they are no longer able to sustain themselves at their new levels of consumption. Second, inequalities increase the optimum population size of the community by favoring greater production from a larger number of producers; at the same time, they also lower the living standard of these producers. Finally, inequalities in the distribution and consumption of energy often lead to new patterns of consumption. As the wealthy individuals use more luxury goods or rely increasingly on services performed by others, a new pattern of occupations can emerge in the community. The wealthy help to create new kinds of jobs tied closely to their status. These new jobs reinforce existing inequalities and can lead to further increases in both the real and optimum populations of the community.

The adoption of technological or organizational innovations can change not only the amount of energy produced in a community but also the ways in which it is produced and consumed. Suppose that by adopting a particular innovation, the same number of individuals, working the same number of hours, can produce twice as much energy as they did previously. This raises the living standard of their community and the size of its maximum population—the largest number of people that can be supported using the new technology as efficiently as possible and distributing the energy produced equally to all members of the group. However, the optimum population size of this community can either rise or fall, depending on the kind of innovation that was adopted and what happens when a new member is added to the labor force. In other words, the marginal productivity of the community plays an important role in determining just how beneficial the new innovation will be in the long run. Not all innovations are equally beneficial. The adoption of some innovations may actually lower energy production in the community and hence its standard of living. Other innovations may raise the community's living standard when it has one population and lower it when it is composed of a greater or lesser number of individuals.

So far, we have treated the relationships between population and economy as if the community existed in isolation or the effects of external trade were neutral. Usually neither is the case. External trade brings energy into the community in the form of the goods and services its members acquire from outsiders. At the same time, it takes energy away from the community, as its members provide goods and services to other groups. Changes in the extent or direction of external trade are equivalent, in one sense, to the kinds of changes that result from technological and organizational innovations. They can alter the living standard of the community and change the sizes of its optimum and maximum populations.

DIVERSITY AND DEVELOPMENT IN CHANGING ENVIRONMENTS

One of the more fascinating features of America's past is the tremendous diversity we see in the archaeological record. Cultural diversity was already apparent before the end of the Pleistocene Epoch and has maintained itself to the present day. We have already seen that contemporary communities living in different areas often had very different life styles. We have also seen that the same generalized behavior patterns—for example, agricultural production—often developed in very different ways in different environmental settings. Let us now briefly raise two questions. What has produced and maintained this diversity? And what has limited its range of variation?

Human communities have adapted their behavior to the kinds of social and natural environments where they live. These adaptations are reflected in many aspects of their behavior—not only in those elements that we tend to think of as being strictly economic but also in those elements like kinship and religion that we tend to view as having very little to do with economy. Every community employs a set of strategies for acquiring what its members need from their surroundings at a particular time. Strategies that are very well adapted for life in one environmental setting may be completely inappropriate for life in another setting. As a result, communities living in different situations often employ very different strategies for satisfying their wants.

It is even conceivable that two groups living in exactly the same setting might use very different strategies because of their perceptions of the environment and their past experiences.

We have also seen that the social and natural environments of a community are continually changing. In the short run, there are seasonal and annual fluctuations in the availability and abundance of many of the items that the community needs. In the long run, some of these items may eventually disappear altogether while others become more plentiful. This variation is produced by several factors—changes in the physical environment, the activities of the community itself, and the effects that other peoples have on its members. All communities have to deal with variable environments; however, the amount of variation they have to cope with may differ considerably in both time and space.

Adaptive strategies are designed to deal with the environmental conditions that exist at a particular moment in time. However, the problem is to recognize exactly what the existing conditions are. By the time a community has worked out and refined a set of strategies reasonably well adapted to the conditions its members perceive, the environment may have changed, and their strategies may no longer be very well suited in the new situation. When this happens, the effectiveness of their adaptation, or fitness, to the environment diminishes. The community is no longer behaving in the most efficient ways for the purpose of sustaining itself. The danger in this situation increases with the length of the time lag between the environmental change and the adoption of the new strategies. This is true not only for hunting and gathering communities but also for the highly industrialized nations of the world, like the United States or the U.S.S.R., that must eventually deal with the consequences of pollution, alienation, and resource depletion on a global scale—to name only a few of the problems they have created for themselves and for the rest of mankind.

Optimistically, communities adopt new strategies once they recognize that their environments have changed and that the old strategies are no longer working as efficiently as they did earlier. However, recognizing that a situation has changed is not always a simple process. It involves interpreting a complex set of information provided by past experience, taste, and the environment itself. Furthermore, it is a highly selective process. Certain pieces of information are accepted as important and are emphasized at the expense of those data that tend to reinforce the older views.

The complexity of this information and the selectivity that a community employs in interpreting it have two important consequences. First, there is no necessary relationship between the kinds of information a community will choose to consider and the ways in which its members will ultimately respond to the situation that has emerged. Old strategies may be retained or new ones adopted provided that the cost of following them seems to be offset by the benefits they bring to the community as a whole. The long-term effects of any response can be either advantageous or deleterious, depending on how each of them affects the community's effectiveness in the new situation. Second, decisions to use one set of data in interpreting the new situation instead of another also affect a community's adaptation and fitness to its environment. They limit the range of alternative responses that are potentially available to the group. Its members can only consider adopting those strategy sets they see as appropriate for the new environmental setting; they must reject the other possibilities. In doing so, they are opening up the possibilities for following some developmental pathways and are blocking the possibilities for following other routes.

The kinds and number of responses that are available to a community also affect the ability of its members to cope effectively with a new situation. The reasons for this are fairly clear. Different responses to the same situation are not always equally beneficial; some of them may increase the group's fitness to its new environment much more than others do. In selecting the optimum response to the new situation, the community will want to adopt those strategy sets that maximize its fitness as quickly and easily as possible and will want to reject the others. In general, groups that have a large number of possible responses to choose from probably have a greater chance of eventually maximizing their fitness than those that have only one or two alternatives open to them.

It is useful to view the past in terms of the adaptive strategies employed by different communities at various times in their histories to deal with changes in their social and natural environments. The way a particular community responds at any given time depends not only on the characteristics of its members at that moment but also on the kind of environmental change that has taken place. At another time in its history, the same group might respond very differently to the same set of circumstances. What we are looking at in a microcosm is a huge reservoir of variation that has continually produced and maintained the diversity we see in the archaeological record. The adaptive strategies employed at various times in the past are ultimately based on this variation, and, depending on their effectiveness in a wide range of environmental settings, they have imposed limits on the kinds of diversity that have appeared. Communities tend to retain those strategies that work well or adopt new ones that work well for someone else.

There is another aspect to the diversity we see in the archaeological record. It is concerned with the historical sequences of events and the behavioral patterns that have emerged as responses to the conditions imposed by these events. Because archaeologists usually work out the particular details of what happened in relatively small areas, there are many of these temporal sequences, or lines of development, in the New World. When they are compared with each other, we are immediately struck by their diversity. No two of them are quite the same, and, the farther away the two are from each other, the greater the differences they are likely to exhibit. Some lines show almost continual change, while others show virtually no change at all. Some lines seem to diverge almost continually, while others seem to become more similar. We can account for some of this in terms of adaptations to particular environmental situations.

A community that has already maximized its fitness to a stable environment can maintain itself indefinitely, simply by continuing to use the same strategies for acquiring what it needs. There are even a few examples of this in the archaeological record, as on the south coast of Chile, where the earliest known inhabitants of the area worked out a set of adaptive responses based on littoral harvesting and canoe transportation. As recently as 1942, many of the people in the area were still using these techniques in virtually the same ways their predecessors had. In a variable environment—regardless of whether the changes occur regularly or only sporadically—a community is continually exposed to new pressures that reduce its fitness. In order to regain what they have lost, the members of this group must eventually adopt new strategies if they are to survive. This process has occurred many times in the New World. We have already examined in considerable detail what happened when the inhabitants of the Tehuacán Valley in Mexico decided to spend a little more time each year in harvesting wild grasses. This seemingly insignificant change in their activities ultimately had enormous effects on the daily lives of their descendants and on the social and natural environments in which they lived.

Lines of development also show varying degrees of convergence and divergence. Convergence occurs in those situations where different communites find it most advantageous to adopt roughly the same strategy sets in order to deal efficiently with the environmental pressures that confront them. These responses often have very different antecedents in the various lines of development that are being considered. It appears that certain broad responses—such as agricultural production or multi-community forms of organization—have proven time and again to be particularly effective ways of dealing with a wide range of environmental pressures. Divergence occurs in those situations where different communities find it more convenient to adopt alternative strategy sets to cope with new environmental conditions. This is especially evident when we look at the kinds of adaptations that have developed among contemporary populations or settlements in the same small area.

We have not yet begun to solve all of the problems in American archaeology, let alone even ask the kinds of questions that will allow us to formulate new problems more clearly. In the preceding pages, we have examined a few selected problems in American archaeology and some of their implications. By asking new questions, new kinds of information become important and deficiencies in the earlier work apparent. As new information becomes available, the conclusions, interpretations, and speculations presented here will undoubtedly be modified and enhanced as our understanding of what happened increases. It is the process of trying to solve these and other problems that makes American archaeology a constantly changing, controversial, and growing field for investigation. Like history and other fields of study that are concerned mainly with what happened in the past, American archaeology can tell us something about the present, if we will only take the time to ponder the lessons it provides.

A Bibliographical Essay

Footnotes have been avoided throughout the book to ensure some degree of reading continuity. The following essay remedies this deficiency by providing references for those who want to read more on the topics discussed.

1. WHAT IS ARCHAEOLOGY?

John Rowe describes what is involved in becoming an archaeologist in "Archaeology as a Career," *Archaeology* 7 (no. 3, 1954): 229–36. Many authors have discussed how the archaeologist deals with his evidence; some of the more useful ones are V. Gordon Childe, *Piecing Together the Past; The Interpretation of Archaeological Data* (New York, Praeger Publishers, Inc., 1956); James Deetz, *Invitation to Archaeology* (New York, Doubleday & Company, Inc., 1967); Frank Hole and Robert Heizer, *An Introduction to Prehistoric Archaeology* (New York, Holt Rinehart & Winston, Inc., 1969); Robert Heizer and John Graham, *A Guide to Field Methods in Archaeology* (Palo Alto, National Press Books, 1967); and Mortimer Wheeler, *Archaeology from the Earth* (Baltimore, Penguin Books Inc., 1956).

Examples of anthropologists and historians who can use data from each other's field are Marc Bloch, *French Rural Society; An Essay on Its Basic Characteristics* (Berkeley, University of California Press, 1966); Sherburne Cook, "The Historical Demography and Ecology of Teotlalpan," *Ibero-Americana:* 33 and "Soil Erosion and Population in Central Mexico," *Ibero-Americana:* 34 (Berkeley and Los Angeles, University of California Press, 1949); Moses Finley, *The World of Odysseus: Homer and His Age in Archaeology, Literature, and History* (New York, World Publishing Company, Meridian Books, 1959); Lynn White, *Medieval Technology and Social Change* (Oxford, The Clarendon Press, 1962); Eric Wolf, *Sons of the Shaking Earth*

(Chicago, University of Chicago Press, 1959); and John Murra, "An Archaeological 'Restudy' of an Andean Ethnohistorical Account," *American Antiquity* 28 (no. 1, 1962): 1–4.

The interpretation of archaeological evidence is discussed by John Rowe, "Archaeological Dating and Cultural Process," *Southwestern Journal of Anthropology* 15 (no. 4, 1959): 317–24; John Rowe, "Stratigraphy and Seriation," *American Antiquity* 26 (no. 3, 1961): 324–30; John Rowe, "Stages and Periods in Archaeological Interpretation," *Southwestern Journal of Anthropology* 18 (no. 1, 1962): 40–54; John Rowe, "Worsaae's Law and the Use of Grave Lots for Archaeological Dating," *American Antiquity* 28 (no. 2, 1962): 129–37; and Thomas Patterson, "Contemporaneity and Cross-dating in Archaeological Interpretation," *American Antiquity* 28 (no. 3, 1963): 389–92.

Tree-ring dating is discussed by Bryan Bannister, "Dendrochronology," *Science in Archaeology*, edited by Donald Brothwell and Eric Higgs, pp. 162–76 (London, Thames & Hudson Ltd., 1963) and "The Interpretation of Tree-ring Dates," *American Antiquity* 27 (no. 4, 1962): 508–14.

The Maya calendar is described by Sylvanus Morley, *The Ancient Maya*, 3rd ed., revised by George Brainerd (Stanford, Stanford University Press, 1956), pp. 230–49 and J. Eric Thompson, *The Rise and Fall of Maya Civilization*, 2nd ed. (Norman, Oklahoma, University of Oklahoma Press, 1966), pp. 162–83. The correlation of the Maya calendar with the Christian one has recently been examined by Linton Satterwaite and Elizabeth Ralph, "New Radiocarbon Dates and the Maya Correlation Problem," *American Antiquity* 26 (no. 2, 1960): 165-84.

The radiocarbon dating method is described by Willard Libby, *Radiocarbon Dating*, 2nd ed. (Chicago, University of Chicago Press, 1955) and W. S. Broecker and J. L. Kulp, "The Radiocarbon Method of Age Determination," *American Antiquity* 22 (no. 1, 1956): 1-11. The limitations of the method are described by T. Rafter and G. Fergusson, "The Atom Bomb Effect; Recent Increase in the ^{14}C Content of the Atmosphere, Biosphere, and Surface Waters of the Oceans," *New Zealand Journal of Science and Technology* 38 (no. 8, 1957): 871–83; Hans Suess, "Radiocarbon Concentration in Modern Wood," *Science* 122 (no. 3166, 1955): 415–16 and "Secular Variations of the Cosmic-ray-produced Carbon 14 in the Atmosphere and Their Interpretations," *Journal of Geophysical Research* 70 (no. 23, 1965): 5937–52; T. Rafter, "^{14}C Variations in Nature and the Effect on Radiocarbon Dating," *New Zealand Journal of Science and Technology* 37 (no. 1, 1955): 20–38; Edward Deevey *et al.*, "The Natural C^{14} Contents of Materials from Hard-water Lakes," *Proceedings of the National Academy of Sciences* 40, no. 5

(Washington, 1954): 285–88; Robert Hall, "Those Late Corn Cobs; Isotopic Fractionization as a Source of Error in Carbon-14 Dating" (Paper presented at the annual meeting of the Central States Anthropological Society, Chicago, 1967); John Rowe, "An Interpretation of Radiocarbon Measurements on Archaeological Samples from Peru," *Proceedings of the Sixth International Conference, Radiocarbon and Tritium Dating,* compiled by Roy Chatters and Edwin Olson (Springfield, Va., 1966), pp. 187–98; and Robert Stuckenrath, "The Care and Feeding of Radiocarbon Dates," *Archaeology* 18 (no. 3, 1965): 277–81.

2. THE EARLY AMERICANS

Standard works dealing with the Pleistocene world are Richard Flint, *Glacial and Quaternary Geology* (New York, John Wiley & Sons, Inc., 1971); H. E. Wright, Jr., and David Frey, eds., *The Quaternary of the United States* (Princeton, N.J., Princeton University Press, 1965); and E. J. Cushing and H. E. Wright, Jr., eds., *Quaternary Paleoecology* (New Haven, Conn., Yale University Press, 1967).

The modern environments of the New World and their distribution are described by Victor Shelford, *The Ecology of North America* (Urbana, Ill., University of Illinois Press, 1963) and E. J. Fittkau *et al., Biogeography and Ecology in South America,* 2 vols. (The Hague, Dr. W. Junk, 1968–1969). An easy introduction to meteorology is provided in Vernon Finch and Glenn Trewartha, *Elements of Geography: Physical and Cultural* (New York, McGraw-Hill Book Company, 1949), pp. 26–216. Glenn Trewartha, *The Earth's Problem Climates* (Madison, Wis., University of Wisconsin Press, 1966) discusses the contemporary climates of the New World and the meteorological conditions that produce them.

Derek Ager, *Principles of Paleoecology: An Introduction to the Study of How and Where Animals and Plants Lived in the Past* (New York, McGraw-Hill Book Company, 1963) describes how ancient environments are reconstructed. Late Pleistocene climates and their effects on the distribution of major environmental zones in the New World are examined by Reid Bryson and Wayne Wendland, "Tentative Climatic Patterns for Some Late Glacial and Post-glacial Episodes in Central North America," *Life, Land, and Water; Proceedings of the 1966 Conference on Environmental Studies of the Glacial Lake Agassiz Region,* edited by William Mayer-Oakes, pp. 271–98 (Winnipeg, The University of Manitoba Press, 1967); Hurd Willett, "The General Circulation at the Last (Würm) Glacial Maximum," *Geografiska Annaler* 32 (Häfte 3–4, Stockholm, 1950): 179–87; and Thomas C. Patterson and Edward P. Lanning, "Los Medios Ambientes Glacial Tardío y Postglacial de Sudamerica," *Boletín de la Sociedad Geográfica de Lima* LXXXVI (Lima, 1967), pp. 1–19.

S. Jelgersma, "Sea-level Changes During the Last 10,000 Years," *Proceedings of the International Symposium on World Climate, 8000 to 0 B.C.*, edited by J. S. Sawyer (London, Royal Meteorological Society, 1966), pp. 54–71 evaluates the various interpretations of sea level change in postglacial times. Recent evidence concerning the extent and timing of sea level changes during the Pleistocene are examined by Kenneth Emery and Louis Garrison, "Sea Levels 7,000 to 20,000 Years Ago" *Science* 157 (no. 3789, 1967): 684–87 and John Milliman and Kenneth Emery, "Sea Levels During the Past 35,000 Years," *Science* 162 (no. 3858, 1968): 1121–23.

Margaret Davis, "Phytogeography and Palynology of Northeastern United States," *The Quaternary of the United States*, edited by H. E. Wright, Jr., and David Frey (Princeton, N.J., Princeton University Press, 1967), pp. 377–401 describes the sequence of plant communities from late glacial times to the present in New England. Gerald Schultz, "Four Superimposed Late-Pleistocene Vertebrate Faunas from Southwest Kansas," *Pleistocene Extinctions; The Search for a Cause*, edited by Paul Martin and H. E. Wright, Jr. (New Haven, Conn., Yale University Press, 1967), pp. 321–37 describes the late glacial environment of that area.

There is a rapidly growing body of literature on the extinction of large animals during the Pleistocene and its causes, much of which is summarized in Paul Martin and H. E. Wright, Jr., eds. *Pleistocene Extinctions; The Search for a Cause* (New Haven, Conn., Yale University Press, 1967). Grover Krantz, "Human Activities and Megafaunal Extinction," *American Scientist* 58 (no. 2, 1970): 164–70 presents a new stimulating approach to the whole problem.

The twenty-four papers in David Hopkins, ed., *The Bering Land Bridge* (Stanford, Stanford University Press, 1967) examine various aspects of the natural history and anthropology of that region. Information on journeying across the ice fields of the Bering Straits at the present time comes from Richard MacNeish who got it from Diamond Jenness, who, as far as is known, is the only anthropologist who ever spent the winter around the Bering Straits.

The following papers summarize the evidence for the antiquity of man in the New World: Alan Bryan, "Early Man in America and the Late Pleistocene Chronology of Western Canada and Alaska," *Current Anthropology* 10 (no. 4, 1969): 339–65; Ruth Gruhn, "The Archaeology of Wilson Butte Cave, South-Central Idaho," *Occasional Papers of the Idaho State Museum* no. 6

(Pocatello, 1961); Cynthia Irwin-Williams, "Associations of Early Man with Horse, Camel, and Mastodon at Hueyatlaco, Valsequillo (Puebla, Mexico)," *Pleistocene Extinctions; The Search for a Cause,* edited by Paul Martin and H. E. Wright, Jr. (New Haven, Conn., Yale University Press, 1967), pp. 337–48; Irving Rouse and José Cruxent, *Venezuelan Archaeology* (New Haven, Conn., Yale University Press, 1963); Richard S. MacNeish *et al., Second Annual Report of the Ayacucho Archaeological-Botanical Project* (Andover, Mass., Robert S. Peabody Foundation for Archaeology, 1970); Richard MacNeish, "Early Man in the Andes," *Scientific American* 224 (no. 4, 1971): 36–46; Thomas Patterson, "Early Cultural Remains on the Central Coast of Peru," *Ñawpa Pacha* 4 (1966): 145–53; Edward Lanning and Thomas Patterson, "Early Man in South America," *Scientific American* 217 (no. 5, 1967): 44–50; Edward Lanning, "Ayacucho-Exacto Comparisons" (New York, unpublished manuscript, 1970); Junius Bird, "Antiquity and Migration of the Early Inhabitants of Patagonia," *The Geographical Review,* XXVIII (no. 2, 1938): 250–75; James Millar, *Archaeology of Fisherman Lake, Western District of Mackenzie, N.W.T.* (Unpublished Ph.D. Dissertation, Calgary, University of Calgary, Department of Archaeology, 1968); and Alex Krieger, "Early Man in the New World," *Prehistoric Man in the New World,* edited by Jesse Jennings and Edward Norbeck (Chicago, University of Chicago Press, 1964), pp. 23–81.

The various techniques for making stone tools are discussed in detail by S. A. Semenov, *Prehistoric Technology; An Experimental Study of the Oldest Tools and Artefacts from Traces of Manufacture and Wear* (London, Cory, Adams & Mackay, Ltd., 1964); Don Crabtree, "Notes on Experiments in Flint Knapping: 1 Heat Treatment of Silica Materials," *Tebiwa* 7 (no. 1, 1964): 1–6; "A Stoneworker's Approach to Analyzing and Replicating the Lindenmeier Folsom," *Tebiwa* 9 (no. 1, 1966): 3–39; "Notes on Experiments in Flint Knapping: 3 The Flintknapper's Raw Materials," *Tebiwa* 10 (no. 1, 1967): 8–24; "Notes on Experiments in Flint Knapping: 4 Tools Used for Making Flaked Stone Artefacts," *Tebiwa* 10 (no. 1, 1967): 60–72; "Mesoamerican Polyhedral Cores and Prismatic Blades," *American Antiquity* 33 (no. 4, 1968): 446–78; and "Flaking Stone with Wooden Implements," *Science* 169 (no. 3941, 1970): 146–53; François Bordes and Don Crabtree, "The Corbiac Blade Technique and Other Experiments," *Tebiwa* 12 (no. 2, 1969): 1–21; and Jacques Bordaz, *Tools of the Old and New Stone Age* (Garden City, N.J., The Natural History Press, 1970).

Hans-Georg Bandi, *Eskimo Prehistory* (Seattle, University of Washington Press, 1968) summarizes much of the literature dealing with Arctic archaeology. The discussion in this book is based on Richard MacNeish, "Investigations in Southwest Yukon," *Papers of the Robert S. Peabody Foundation for Archaeology* 6, no. 2 (Andover, Mass., 1964); Frederick Hadleigh-West, "The Donnelly Ridge Site and the Definition of an Early Core and Blade Complex in Central Alaska," *American Antiquity* 32 (no. 3, 1967): 360–82; Douglas Anderson, "A Stone Age Campsite at the Gateway to America," *Scientific American* 218 (no. 6, 1968): 24–33; and James Millar, *Archaeology of Fisherman Lake, Western District of Mackenzie, N.W.T.* (Unpublished Ph.D. Dissertation, Calgary, University of Calgary, Department of Archaeology, 1968). The relationships between the American Arctic, Japan, and northeast Asia are examined by Kensaku Hayashi, "The Fuqui Microblade Technology and Its Relationship to Northeast Asia and North America," *Arctic Anthropology* V (no. 1, 1968): 128–90.

The following works provide a useful summary of late glacial and early postglacial archaeology: George MacDonald, "Debert: A Palaeo-Indian Site in Central Nova Scotia," *Anthropological Papers of the National Museum of Canada* no. 16 (Ottawa, 1968); Henry Irwin, *The Itama: Late Pleistocene Inhabitants of the Plains of the United States and Canada and the American Southwest* (Unpublished Ph.D. Dissertation, Cambridge, Mass., Harvard University Department of Anthropology, 1967); David Browman and David Munsell, "Columbia Plateau Prehistory: Cultural Development and Impinging Influences," *American Antiquity* 34 (no. 3, 1969): 249–64; Vance Haynes, "Fluted Projectile Points, Their Age and Dispersion," *Science* 145 (no. 3639, 1964): 1408–13; and Claude Warren and Anthony Ranere, "Outside Danger Cave: A View of Early Man in the Great Basin," *Early Man in Western North America,* edited by Cynthia Irwin-Williams (Portales, N.M., Eastern New Mexico University Press, 1968), pp. 6–18.

Joseph Birdsell, "Some Population Problems Involving Pleistocene Man," *Cold Spring Harbor Symposia on Quantitative Biology* 22 (Cold Spring Harbor, 1957), pp. 47–69 provides information on population growth rates when groups move into previously unoccupied areas. The relationship between resources and population is examined by Edward Ackerman, "Population and Natural Resources," *The Study of Population; An Inventory and Appraisal,* edited by Philip Hauser and Otis Dudley (Chicago, University of Chicago Press, 1959), pp. 621–48. Kent Flannery, "The Postglacial 'Readaptation' as Viewed from Mesoamerica," *American Antiquity* 31 (no. 6, 1966): 800–806 and James Fitting, "Environmental Potential and the Postglacial Readaptation in Eastern North America," *American Antiquity* 33 (no. 4, 1968): 441–45 examine the kinds of environmental changes and cultural adjustments that occurred in two different regions in early postglacial times.

3. THE EMERGENCE OF FOOD PRODUCTION

Gordon Willey, *An Introduction to American Archaeology*, 2 vols. (Englewood Cliffs, N.J., Prentice-Hall, Inc., 1966 and 1971) summarizes the early postglacial archaeology of the New World. The discussion here is based on Joseph Caldwell, "Trend and Tradition in the Prehistory of the Eastern United States," *American Anthropological Association Memoir*, no. 88 (Menasha, 1958); James Fitting, "Scheduling in a Shared Environment: Late Period Land Use Patterns in the Saginaw Valley of Michigan" (Unpublished Paper Presented at the Annual Meeting of the Society for American Archaeology, Milwaukee, 1969); Lewis Napton, "The Lacustrine Subsistence Pattern in the Desert West," *The Kroeber Anthropological Society Papers, Special Publication*, no. 2 (Berkeley, 1969), pp. 28–98; Kent Flannery, "Archaeological Systems Theory and Early Mesoamerica," *Anthropological Archeology in the Americas*, edited by Betty Meggers (Washington, The Anthropological Society of Washington, 1968), pp. 67–87; Edward Lanning, "Early Man in Peru," *Scientific American* 213 (no. 4, 1965): 68–76; Thomas Patterson and Michael Moseley, "Late Preceramic and Early Ceramic Cultures of the Central Coast of Peru," *Ñawpa Pacha* 6 (1968): 115–34; and Thomas Patterson, "The Emergence of Food Production in Central Peru," *Prehistoric Agriculture*, edited by Stuart Struever (Garden City, N.Y., The Natural History Press, 1971), pp. 181–207.

The relationship between population pressure and the intensity of land use is examined in detail by Ester Boserup, *The Conditions of Agricultural Growth; The Economics of Agrarian Change under Population Pressure* (Chicago, Aldine Publishing Company, 1965).

Corn domestication is examined by Paul Mangelsdorf *et al.*, "Prehistoric Wild and Cultivated Maize," *The Prehistory of the Tehuacán Valley*, vol. 1, edited by Douglas Byers (Austin, Texas, University of Texas Press, 1967), pp. 178–200; Alexander Grobman *et al.*, "Races of Maize in Peru," *National Academy of Sciences and National Research Council Publication*, no. 915 (Washington, 1961); and David Kelley and Duccio Bonavia, "New Evidence for Pre-ceramic Maize on the Coast of Peru," *Ñawpa Pacha* 1 (1963): 33–42.

The domestication process is examined by C. D. Darlington, *Chromosome Botany and the Origin of Cultivated Plants* (New York, Hafner Publishing Co., Inc., 1963); Edgar Anderson, *Plants, Man and Life* (Berkeley, University of California Press, 1969); Verne Grant, *The Origins of Adaptations* (New York, Columbia University Press, 1963); Ramón Margalef, *Perspectives in Ecological Theory* (Chicago, University of Chicago Press,

1968); and David Harris, "Agricultural Systems, Ecosystems and the Origins of Agriculture," J. G. Hawkes, "The Ecological Background of Plant Domestication," and Daniel Zohary, "The Progenitors of Wheat and Barley in Relation to Domestication and Agricultural Dispersal in the Old World," all of which are published in *The Domestication and Exploitation of Plants and Animals,* edited by Peter Ucko and G. W. Dimbleby (Chicago, Aldine Publishing Company, 1969).

The beginnings of agricultural economies in various parts of the world are discussed by Lewis Binford, "Post-Pleistocene Adaptations," *New Perspectives in Archeology,* edited by Sally Binford and Lewis Binford (Chicago, Aldine Publishing Company, 1968), pp. 313–41; Kent Flannery, "The Ecology of Early Food Production in Mesopotamia," *Science* 147 (no. 3663, 1965): 1247–56; Kent Flannery, "Origins and Ecological Effects of Early Domestication in Iran and the Near East," *The Domestication and Exploitation of Plants and Animals,* edited by Peter Ucko and G. W. Dimbleby (Chicago, Aldine Publishing Company, 1969), pp. 73–102; and Kent Flannery, "Archaeological Systems Theory and Early Mesoamerica," *Anthropological Archeology in the Americas,* edited by Betty Meggers (Washington, The Anthropological Society of Washington, 1968), pp. 67–87; Carl Sauer, *Agricultural Origins and Dispersals,* 2nd ed. (Cambridge, The M.I.T. Press, 1969); and various essays in *Prehistoric Agriculture,* edited by Stuart Struever (Garden City, N.Y., The Natural History Press, 1971).

The development of agricultural production in the Tehuacán Valley is dealt with by *The Prehistory of the Tehuacán Valley,* edited by Douglas Byers (Austin, Texas, University of Texas Press, 1967); Richard MacNeish, *First Annual Report of the Tehuacan Archaeological-Botanical Project* (Andover, Mass., Robert S. Peabody Foundation for Archaeology, 1961); Richard MacNeish, *Second Annual Report of the Tehuacan Archaeological-Botanical Project* (Andover, Mass., Robert S. Peabody Foundation for Archaeology, 1962); Richard MacNeish, "Ancient Mesoamerican Civilization," *Science* 143 (3606, 1964): 531–37; Richard MacNeish, "The Origins of New World Civilization," *Scientific American* 211 (no. 5, 1964): 29–37; Richard MacNeish, "The Scheduling Factor in the Development of Effective Food Production in the Tehuacan Valley" (Unpublished Manuscript, Andover, Mass., no date); Richard MacNeish, "Social Implications and Changes in Population and Settlement of the 12,000 Years of Prehistory in the Tehuacan Valley of Mexico (Unpublished Manuscript, Andover, Mass., 1968); Richard MacNeish, "The Evolution of Community Patterns in the Tehuacan Valley of Mexico and Speculations about the Cultural Processes" (Unpublished Manuscript, 1970); and Richard MacNeish "Speculations about How and Why Food Production and Village Life Developed in the Tehuacan Valley, Mexico," *Archaeology* 24 (no. 4, 1971): 307–15; Earle Smith, "Agriculture, Tehuacán Valley," *Fieldiana: Botany* 31 (no. 3, 1965); Earle Smith, "Flora, Tehuacán Valley," *Fieldiana: Botany* 31 (no. 4, 1965); and Karen Stothert, "A Reinterpretation of Subsistence Information from the Tehuacán Valley" (Unpublished Manuscript, New Haven, Conn., Yale University, Department of Anthropology, 1969).

The spread of innovations is examined by Gwyn Jones, "The Diffusion of Agricultural Innovations," *Journal of Agricultural Economics* XV (3, 1963): 387–405; Everett Rogers, *Diffusion of Innovations* (New York, The Free Press, 1962); Herbert Lionberger, *Adoption of New Ideas and Practices* (Ames, Iowa, Iowa State University Press, 1960); National Science Foundation, "Diffusion of Technological Change," *Readings in Resource Management and Conservation,* edited by Ian Burton and Robert Kates (Chicago, University of Chicago Press, 1965), pp. 493–501; L. A. Brown and E. G. Moore, "Diffusion Research in Geography: A Perspective," *Progress in Geography,* edited by Christopher Board *et al.,* vol. 1 (London, Edward Arnold (Publishers) Ltd., 1969), pp. 119–57; Homer Barnett, "Diffusion Rates," *Process and Pattern in Culture; Essays in Honor of Julian H. Steward,* edited by Robert Manners (Chicago, Aldine Publishing Company, 1964), pp. 351–63; and Margaret Hodgen, "Change and History," *Viking Fund Publications in Anthropology* no. 18 (1952).

The development of food production on the central coast of Peru is discussed by Edward Lanning, "Early Man in Peru," *Scientific American* 213 (no. 4, 1965): 68–76; Michael Moseley, *Changing Subsistence Patterns: Late Preceramic Archaeology of the Central Peruvian Coast* (Unpublished Ph.D. Dissertation, Cambridge, Mass., Harvard University, Department of Anthropology, 1968); Thomas Patterson, "The Emergence of Food Production in Central Peru," *Prehistoric Agriculture,* edited by Stuart Struever, (Garden City, N.Y., Natural History Press, 1971), pp. 181–207; Thomas Patterson, "Central Peru: Its Population and Economy," *Archaeology* 24 (no. 4, 1971): 316–21; Thomas Patterson and Edward Lanning, "Changing Settlement Patterns on the Central Peruvian Coast," *Ñawpa Pacha* 2 (1964): 113–23; and Thomas Patterson and Michael Moseley, "Late Preceramic and Early Ceramic Cultures of the Central Coast of Peru," *Ñawpa Pacha* 6 (1968): 115–34.

4. SETTLEMENTS

The location of settlements is discussed by Michael Chisholm, *Rural Settlement and Land Use; An Essay in Location* (New

York, John Wiley & Sons, Inc., 1967); William Bunge, "Theoretical Geography," *Lund Studies in Geography*, ser. C (no. 1, 1966); J. A. Everson and B. P. FitzGerald, *Settlement Patterns* (London, Longmans, Green & Co. Ltd., 1969); Allan Pred, "Behavior and Location; Foundations for a Geographic and Dynamic Location Theory, *"Lund Studies in Geography*, ser. B (no. 27, 1967); Peter Haggett, *Locational Analysis in Human Geography* (London, Edward Arnold (Publishers) Ltd., 1965); and August Lösch, *The Economics of Location* (New York, John Wiley & Sons, Inc., 1967).

Preliminary analyses of the Peruvian data in this section are presented by Edward Lanning, "A Pre-agricultural Occupation on the Central Coast of Peru," *American Antiquity* 28 (no. 3, 1963): 360–71; Edward Lanning, "Early Man in Peru," *Scientific American* 213 (no. 4, 1965): 68–76; Thomas Patterson, "The Emergence of Food Production in Central Peru," *Prehistoric Agriculture*, edited by Stuart Struever (Garden City, N.Y., Natural History Press, 1971), pp. 181–207; and Thomas Patterson, "Central Peru: Its Population and Economy," *Archaeology* 24 (no. 4, 1971): 316–321.

Karen Spalding, *Indian Rural Society in Colonial Peru: The Example of Huarochirí* (Unpublished Ph.D. Dissertation, Berkeley, University of California, Department of History, 1967) and Thomas Patterson and Karen Spalding, "The Archaeology and Ethnohistory of the San Pedro de Mama Region" (Unpublished Manuscript, Lima, 1968) discuss the changes in settlement patterns and socioeconomic conditions in the middle Rimac Valley. Eugene McDougle, "Notes on Pachacamac" (Unpublished Manuscript, Pachacamac, 1968–1971) and Thomas Patterson "The Oracle and the Inca: The Role of Pachacamac in Andean Culture History" (Unpublished Paper presented at the Annual Meeting of the Society for American Archaeology, Reno, 1967) discuss the influence of the oracle at Pachacamac. The most detailed discussion of innovations and their significance is Homer Barnett, *Innovation; The Basis of Culture Change* (New York, McGraw-Hill Book Company, 1957).

The internal structure of Tenochtitlán is examined by Edward Calnek "Urbanization at Tenochtitlán" (Unpublished Paper presented at the Annual Meeting of the American Anthropological Association, New Orleans, 1969); Edward Calnek, "The Internal Structure of Cities: The Case of Tenochtitlán" (Unpublished Paper presented at the XXXIX International Congress of Americanists, Lima, 1970); and Edward Calnek, "Settlement Patterns and Chinampa Agriculture at Tenochtitlán," *American Antiquity* 37 (no. 1, 1972): 104–15. John Rowe, "What Kind of Settlement Was Inca Cuzco?" *Ñawpa Pacha* 5 (1967): 59–76 examines the internal structure of Cuzco.

Preliminary discussions of Teotihuacán are found in René Millon, "The Beginnings of Teotihuacán," *American Antiquity* 26 (no. 1, 1960): 1–10; René Millon, "Cronología y Periodificación; Datos Estratigráficos sobre Períodos Cerámicos y Sus Relaciones con la Pintura Mural," *Teotihuacán; Onceava Mesa Redonda* (Mexico, 1967), pp. 1–18; René Millon "Extensión y Población de la Ciudad de Teotihuacán en Sus Diferentes Períodos; Un Cálculo Provisional," *Teotihuacán; Onceava Mesa Redonda* (Mexico, 1967), pp. 57–78; René Millon "Teotihuacán," *Scientific American* 216 (no. 6, 1967): 38–48; René Millon, "Teotihuacán: Completion of Map of Giant Ancient City in the Valley of Mexico," *Science* 170 (no. 3962, 1970): 1077–82; René Millon *et al.*, "The Pyramid of the Sun at Teotihuacán: 1959 Investigations," *Transactions of the American Philosophical Society* 55, no. 6 (Philadelphia, 1965); and Michael Spence, "The Obsidian Industry of Teotihuacán," *American Antiquity* 32 (no. 4, 1964): 507–14.

Jane Jacobs, *The Economy of Cities* (New York, Random House, Inc., 1969) and Jane Jacobs, *The Death and Life of Great American Cities* (New York, Random House, Inc., 1961) discuss the export multiplier and import replacement effects and the consequences of economic diversity in urban settlements.

J. Beaujeu-Garnier and G. Chabot, *Urban Geography* (London, Longmans, Green & Co. Ltd., 1967) and Arthur Smailes, *The Geography of Towns* (Chicago, Aldine Publishing Company, 1966) discuss town functions and regions. The influence of Teotihuacán on the Valley of Mexico and its environs is examined by Jeffrey Parsons, "Teotihuacán, Mexico and Its Impact on Regional Demography," *Science* 162 (no. 3856, 1968): 872–77 and William Sanders, *The Cultural Ecology of the Teotihuacán Valley* (University Park, Pa., 1965).

5. NATIVE AMERICAN STATES

Frederic Barth, "Introduction," *Ethnic Groups and Boundaries; The Social Organization of Cultural Difference* (Boston, Little, Brown and Company, 1969), pp. 9–38 provides useful insights into recognizing the existence of ethnic groups from archaeological materials. The variation in political systems that existed in Peru before the Inca conquest is described by Dorothy Menzel, "The Inca Occupation of the South Coast of Peru," *Southwestern Journal of Anthropology* 15 (no. 2, 1959): 125–42; Dorothy Menzel and John Rowe, "The Role of Chincha in Late Pre-Spanish Peru," *Ñawpa Pacha* 4 (1966): 63–76; María Rostworowski de Diez Canseco, "Mercaderes del Valle de Chincha en la Epoca Prehispanica: Un Documento y Unos Comentarios," *Revista Española de Antropología Americana* 5 (Madrid, 1970), pp. 135–78; John Rowe, "The Kingdom of Chimor," *Acta Americana* VI (no. 2, Mexico, 1948): 26–59; and John Murra, "An Aymara Kingdom in 1567," *Ethnohistory* 15 (no. 2, 1968): 115–51.

John Murra develops his notion of the vertical archipelago or community self-sufficiency in "Los Cocales Pre-Europeos como Verificación del Modelo de 'Verticalidad' en el Control Ecológico" (Unpublished Paper presented at the XXXIX International Congress of Americanists, Lima, 1970) and Thomas Patterson, "Central Peru: Its Population and Economy," *Archaeology* 24 (no. 4, 1971): 316–21 comments on the application of this concept to populations living on the west slopes of the Peruvian Andes.

Standard works dealing with the ecology of the Andean area are Hans-Wilhelm Koepcke, "Synökologische Studien an der Westseite der peruanischen Anden," *Bonner Geographische Abhandlungen* Heft 29 (Bonn, 1961); Erwin Schweigger, *El Litoral Peruano*, 2nd ed. (Lima, Gráfica Morsom, S.A., 1966); J. A. Tosi, "Zonas de Vida Natural en el Perú," *Instituto Interamericano de Ciencias Agricolas de la OEA Zona Andina, Boletín Tecnico*, no. 5 (Lima, 1966); Carl Troll, "Die geographischen Grundlagen der andinen Kulturen und der Inkareiches," *Ibero-Amerikanischen Archiv* no. 5 (Berlin, 1931): 258–94; and Augusto Weberbauer, *El Mundo Vegetal de los Andes Peruanos* (Lima, Ministerio de Agricultura, 1945).

Statistics issued annually by the Ministry of Agriculture in Peru indicate that agricultural production still varies considerably from one part of the country to another, and studies of contemporary populations show that there are significant regional variations in wealth and level of economic development. A combination of several factors has produced this situation in Peru at the present time; however, there is no reason to assume that analogous patterns of uneven social and economic development did not exist in the past as well. William Isbell, "Potatoes, Corn, and Irrigated Terraces: An Ecological View of Central Andean Prehistory" (Unpublished Paper presented at the Annual Meeting of the American Anthropological Association, Seattle, 1968) shows that there were high-prestige and low-prestige crops in the Andean area at the time of the European invasion and that there were significant regional differences in the amounts of high-prestige crops produced in different regions because of environmental differences. Kent Flannery *et al.*, "Farming Systems and Political Growth in Ancient Oaxaca," *Science* 158 (no. 3800, 1967): 445–54 and Angel Palerm and Eric Wolf, "Ecological Potential and Cultural Development in Mesoamerica," *Social Science Monographs* III (Washington, Pan American Union, 1957), pp. 1–37 show that similar regional differences exist in Mesoamerica as well.

The following papers provide useful information and interpretations of Chavin: John Rowe, "Form and Meaning in Chavin Art," *Peruvian Archaeology; Selected Readings*, edited by John Rowe and Dorothy Menzel (Palo Alto, Peek Publications, 1967), pp. 72–103; John Rowe, "Religion and Empire in Ancient Peru" (Unpublished Paper presented at the Annual Meeting of the Society for American Archaeology, Reno, 1966); and John Rowe, "The Influence of Chavín Art on Later Styles," *Dumbarton Oaks Conference on Chavín*, edited by Elizabeth Benson (Dumbarton Oaks Research Library and Collection, Washington, 1971), pp. 101–24; Luis Lumbreras and Hernan Amat, "Informe Preliminar sobre las Galerias Interiores de Chavín," *Revista del Museo Nacional* XXXIV (Lima, 1969), pp. 143–97; and Thomas Patterson, "Chavín: An Interpretation of Its Spread and Influence," *Dumbarton Oaks Conference on Chavín*, edited by Elizabeth Benson (Dumbarton Oaks Research Library and Collection, Washington, 1971), pp. 29–48.

Janet Siskind, "Tropical Forest Hunters and the Economy of Sex" (Unpublished Paper, New York, 1971) discusses the ideas of economic scarcity and limiting factors. Any discussion of the rise and fall of the Huari state must begin with Dorothy Menzel, "Style and Time in the Middle Horizon," *Ñawpa Pacha* 2 (1964): 1–105; and Dorothy Menzel, "New Data on the Huari Empire in Middle Horizon Epoch 2A," *Ñawpa Pacha* 6 (1968): 47–114 and William Isbell, "Prehistoric Peasants in the Central Andes" (Unpublished Paper presented at the Annual Meeting of the American Anthropological Association, New York, 1971).

The Inca Empire and its organization are described by John Murra, *The Economic Organization of the Inca State* (Unpublished Ph.D. Dissertation, Chicago, University of Chicago, Department of Anthropology, 1956); John Murra, "On Inca Political Structure," *Proceedings of the 1958 Annual Spring Meeting of the American Ethnological Society* (Seattle, 1958), pp. 30–41; John Murra, "Rite and Crop in the Inca State," *Culture and History; Essays in Honor of Paul Radin*, edited by Stanley Diamond (New York, Columbia University Press, 1960), pp. 393–407; John Murra, "Cloth and Its Functions in the Inca State," *American Anthropologist* 64 (no. 4, 1962): 710–28; John Murra, "Herds and Herders in the Inca State," *American Association for the Advancement of Science Publication* no. 78 (Washington, 1965), pp. 185–215; and John Murra, "New Data on Retainer and Servile Populations in Tawantinsuyu," *Actas y Memorias del XXXVI Congreso Internacional de Americanistas* 2 (Seville, 1966), pp. 35–45; María Rostworowski de Diez Canseco, "Succession, Coöption to Kingship, and Royal Incest Among the Inca," *Southwestern Journal of Anthropology* 16 (no. 4, 1960): 417–27; and John Rowe, "Absolute Chronology in the Andean Area," *American Antiquity* X (no. 3, 1945): 265–84; John Rowe, "Inca

Culture at the Time of the Spanish Conquest," *Bureau of American Ethnology Bulletin* 143, vol. 2 (Washington, 1946), pp. 183–331; and John Rowe, "What Kind of Settlement Was Inca Cuzco?" *Ñawpa Pacha* 5 (1967): 59–76.

The importance of markets in Mesoamerica is emphasized by Lee Parsons and Barbara Price, "Mesoamerican Trade and Its Role in the Emergence of Civilization," *Contributions of the University of California Archaeological Facility,* no. 11 (Berkeley, 1971), pp. 169–95.

Recent works on the geography and ecology of Mesoamerica are Robert West, ed., *Handbook of Middle American Indians* vol. 1: *Natural Environment and Early Cultures* (Austin, Texas, University of Texas Press, 1964) and Robert West and John Agelli, *Middle America; Its Lands and Peoples* (Englewood Cliffs, N.J., Prentice-Hall, Inc., 1966).

Useful works on the Olmec include Ignacio Bernal, *The Olmec World* (Berkeley, University of California Press, 1969); Michael Coe, *The Jaguar's Children* (New York, Museum of Primitive Art, 1965); Michael Coe, "The Olmec Style and Its Distribution," *Handbook of Middle American Indians* vol. 3, edited by Robert Wauchope (Austin, Texas, University of Texas Press, 1965), pp. 739–75; and Michael Coe, *America's First Civilization; Discovering the Olmec* (New York, American Heritage Publishing Co., Inc., New York, 1968). David Grove, "The Preclassic Olmec in Central Mexico: Site Distribution and Inferences," *Dumbarton Oaks Conference on the Olmec,* edited by Elizabeth Benson (Dumbarton Oaks Research Library and Collection, Washington, 1968), pp. 179–85 discusses the commercial control center hypothesis, and Kent Flannery, "The Olmec and the Valley of Oaxaca: A Model for Inter-regional Interaction in Formative Times," *Dumbarton Oaks Conference on the Olmec,* edited by Elizabeth Benson (Dumbarton Oaks Research Library and Collection, Washington, 1968), pp. 79–110 formulates the prestige exchange hypothesis. The Olmec occupation of the Gulf Coast is discussed by Michael Coe, "San Lorenzo and the Olmec Civilization," *Dumbarton Oaks Conference on the Olmec,* edited by Elizabeth Benson (Dumbarton Oaks Research Library and Collection, Washington, 1968), pp. 41–78 and Robert Heizer *et al.,* "Investigations at La Venta, 1967," *Contributions of the University of California Archaeological Research Facility,* no. 5 (Berkeley, 1968), pp. 1–34 which also contains a useful bibliography of earlier publications. Paul Tolstoy and Louise Paradis, "Early and Middle Preclassic Culture in the Basin of Mexico," *Science* 167 (no. 3918, 1970): 344–51 examine the Olmec problem from the persepctive of the Valley of Mexico.

The role of trade in the rise of Teotihuacán is examined by Lee

Parsons and Barbara Price, "Mesoamerican Trade and Its Role in the Emergence of Civilization," *Contributions of the University of California Archaeological Research Facility* no. 11 (Berkeley, 1971), pp. 169–95. René Millon, "Trade, Tree Cultivation, and the Development of Private Property in Land," *American Anthropologist* 57 (no. 4, 1955): 698–712 provides information on the importance of cacao and useful inferences about the role it played at Teotihuacán.

The Toltec expansion is examined by Eric Wolf, *Sons of the Shaking Earth* (Chicago, University of Chicago Press, 1959), chapters V and VI; Paul Kirchhoff, "Quetzalcóatl, Huemac y el Fin de Tula," *Cuadernos Americanos* LXXXIV (Mexico, 1955), pp. 163–96; Wigberto Jiménez Moreno, "Síntesis de la Historia Precolonial del Valle de México," *Revista Mexicana de Estudios Antropológicos* XIV (Mexico, 1955), pp. 219–36; and Pedro Armillas, "Northern Mesoamerica," *Prehistoric Man in the New World,* edited by Jesse Jennings and Edward Norbeck (Chicago, University of Chicago Press, 1964), pp. 291–329. Friedrich Katz, *Situación Social y Económica de los Aztecas durante los Siglos XV y XVI* (Mexico, Universidad Nacional Autónoma de México, 1966) provides basic data on the social and economic organization of the Aztec state.

The rise and fall of states are discussed by Robert Carneiro, "A Theory of the Origin of the State," *Science* 169 (no. 3947, 1970): 733–38; Carlo Cipolla, ed., *The Economic Decline of Empires* (London, Methuen & Co. Ltd., 1970), especially pp. 1–15; and Michael Harner, "Population Pressure and the Social Evolution of Agriculturalists," *Southwestern Journal of Anthropology* 26 (no. 1, 1970): 67–86.

6. ECOLOGY, ECONOMY, AND POPULATION

G. Evelyn Hutchinson, "The Concept of Pattern in Ecology," *Proceedings of the Academy of Sciences* 105 (Philadelphia, 1953), pp. 1–12 and G. Evelyn Hutchinson, "Homage to Santa Rosalia or Why Are There so Many Kinds of Animals?" *The American Naturalist* XCIII (1959): 145–59; Robert MacArthur and Joseph Connell, *The Biology of Populations* (New York, John Wiley & Sons, Inc., 1967); and Lawrence Slobodkin, *Growth and Regulation of Animal Populations* (New York, Holt, Rinehart & Winston, Inc., 1966) provide useful discussions of ecology.

Ezra Zubrow, "Carrying Capacity and Dynamic Equilibrium in the Prehistoric Southwest," *American Antiquity* 36 (no. 2, 1971): 127–38 discusses the Hay Hollow Valley in terms of a neo-Malthusian model. James Richardson, "Settlement, Subsistence and Environmental Change in the Talara Region of Northwest Peru, Circa 6000 B.C. to 1500 A.D." (Unpublished Paper presented at the Annual Meeting of the Northeast Anthropological

Society, Albany, 1971) summarizes the data concerning climatic and environmental change on the far north coast of Peru.

The relationship between population and resources is examined by Howard Odum, *Environment, Power, and Society* (New York, John Wiley & Sons, Inc., 1971); Arthur Boughey, *Ecology of Populations* (New York, The Macmillan Company, 1970); D. E. C. Eversley, "Population, Economy, and Society," *Population in History; Essays in Historical Demography*, edited by D. V. Glass and D. E. C. Eversley (London, Edward Arnold (Publishers) Ltd., 1965), pp. 23–69; E. A. Wrigley, *Population and History* (New York, McGraw-Hill Book Company, 1969), especially pp. 61–144; and Alfred Sauvy, *General Theory of Population* (New York, Basic Books, Inc., Publishers, 1969), chapters 1–20. The population of the New World at the time of the European invasion is discussed by Henry Dobyns, "Estimating Aboriginal American Population; An Appraisal of Techniques with a New Hemispheric Estimate," *Current Anthropology* 7 (no. 4, 1966): 395–416.

The problem of dealing with diversity and development in changing environments is dealt with in considerable detail by Richard Levins, *Evolution in Changing Environments; Some Theoretical Explorations* (Princeton, N.J., Princeton University Press, 1968). Adaptations, from a biological perspective, are discussed by George Simpson, *The Major Features of Evolution* (New York, Columbia University Press, 1953) and Verne Grant, *The Origins of Adaptations* (New York, Columbia University Press, 1963). The adaptive strategies of the Alacaluf, who live on the south coast of Chile, are described by Junius Bird, "The Alacaluf," *Bureau of American Ethnology Bulletin* 143, vol. 1 (Washington, 1946), pp. 55–80 and Peter Steager, "The Yaghan and Alacaluf: An Ecological Description," *The Kroeber Anthropological Society Papers*, no. 32 (Berkeley, 1965), pp. 69–76.

FURTHER READINGS ON NEW WORLD ARCHAEOLOGY

The literature dealing with New World archaeology is already enormous, and is growing at an increasing rate each year as more articles, journals, monographs, and books appear on the subject. As a result, it is becoming increasingly difficult to keep track of what is being written. This is particularly true of the periodical literature—where journals appear and disappear each year and articles are published in places where they were never published before. The annual bibliographies of the *Journal de la Société des Américanistes* (Paris) for about the last sixty years are perhaps the single most useful tool for finding out what has been written.

Another method of locating what has been written is based on the fact that most archaeological publications are concerned with particular geographical areas—like Michigan, New York, Colombia, or the American Southwest—that reflect either political boundaries or patterns of archaeological investigation. This technique consists of reading the bibliography of one recent book or article on a particular area, then checking the bibliographies found in each of the references that was cited, and so on.

The bibliography that follows is a highly selective one of a few relatively recent publications with extensive bibliographies. Some general syntheses of New World archaeology are José Alcina Franch, *Manual de Arqueología Americana* (Madrid, Aguilar, 1965); Sally Binford and Lewis Binford, eds., *New Perspectives in Archeology* (Chicago, Aldine Publishing Company, 1968); Geoffrey Bushnell, *The First Americans* (New York, McGraw-Hill Book Company, 1968); Jesse Jennings and Edward Norbeck, *Prehistoric Man in the New World,* edited by Jesse Jennings and Edward Norbeck (Chicago, University of Chicago Press, 1964); George Kubler, *The Art and Architecture of Ancient America* (Baltimore, Penguin Books, 1962); Jonathan Leonard and the Editors of Time-Life Books, *Ancient America* (New York, Time Inc., 1967); Betty Meggers, ed., *Anthropological Archeology in the Americas* (Washington, The Anthropological Society of Washington, 1968); Betty Meggers and Clifford Evans "Aboriginal Cultural Development in Latin America: An Interpretative Review," *Smithsonian Miscellaneous Collection* 146, no. 1 (Washington, 1963); William Sanders and Joseph Marino, *New World Prehistory; Archaeology of the American Indian* (Englewood Cliffs, N.J., Prentice-Hall, Inc., 1970); Gordon Willey, *An Introduction to American Archaeology,* 2 vols. (Englewood Cliffs, N.J., Prentice-Hall, Inc., 1966 and 1971); and Gordon Willey and Philip Phillips, *Method and Theory in American Archaeology* (Chicago, University of Chicago Press, 1958).

Three continental syntheses are Jesse Jennings, *Prehistory of North America* (New York, McGraw-Hill Book Company, 1968); Juan Schobinger, *Prehistoria de Sudamérica* (Barcelona, Editorial Labor, S.A., 1969); and Marie Wormington, *Ancient Man in North America,* 4th ed. (Denver, Denver Museum of Natural History, 1957).

Some regional syntheses of New World archaeology are Hans-Georg Bandi, *Eskimo Prehistory* (Seattle, University of Washington Press, 1968); James Fitting, *The Archaeology of Michigan* (Garden City, N.Y., Natural History Press, 1970); James Griffin, ed., *Archaeology of the Eastern United States* (Chicago, University of Chicago Press, 1952); Alfred Kidder, *An Introduction to the Study of Southwestern Archaeology* (New Haven, Conn., Yale University Press, 1924); William Ritchie, *The Archaeology of New York State* (Garden City, N.Y., Natural History Press, 1965); Claude Baudez, *Central America* (London,

Barrie & Jenkins, 1970); Michael Coe, *Mexico* (New York, Praeger Publishers, Inc., 1962) and *The Maya* (New York, Praeger Publishers, Inc., 1966); Walter Krickeberg, *Altmexikanische Kulturen* (Berlin, Safari-Verlag, 1956); William Sanders and Barbara Price. *Mesoamerica; The Evolution of Civilization* (New York, Random House, Inc., 1968); Eric Wolf, *Sons of the Shaking Earth* (Chicago, University of Chicago Press, 1959); Dick Edgar Ibarra Grasso, *Prehistoria de Bolivia* (Cochabamba, Editorial "Los Amigos del Libro," 1965); Edward Lanning, *Peru Before the Incas* (Englewood Cliffs, N.J., Prentice-Hall, Inc., 1967); Donald Lathrap, *The Upper Amazon* (New York, Praeger Publishers, Inc., 1970); Luis Lumbreras, *De los Pueblos, Las Culturas y Las Artes del Antiguo Perú* (Lima, Moncloa-Campodonico, Editores Asociados, 1969); Betty Meggers, *Ecuador* (New York, Praeger Publishers, Inc., 1966); Gerardo Reichel-Dolmatoff, *Colombia* (New York, Praeger Publishers, Inc., 1965); and Irving Rouse and José Cruxent, *Venezuelan Archaeology* (New Haven, Conn., Yale University Press, 1963).

Index

153

2 3 4 5 6 7 8 9 10 11 12 13 14 15 16 17 18 19 20 21 22 23 24 25   80 79 78 77 76 75 74